TOP 50 SKILLS for a TOP SCORE

ASVAB *Reading and Math

Dr. Janet E. Wall

Mc Graw Hill

New York Chicago San Francisco Lisbon London Madrid Mexico City
Milan New Delhi San Juan Seoul Singapore Sydney Toronto

1 2 3 4 5 6 7 8 9 10 11 12 13 14 15 ROV/ROV 1 9 8 7 6 5 4 3 2 1 0

ISBN: 978-0-07-171801-1
MHID: 0-07-171801-X

LIBRARY OF CONGRESS CONTROL NUMBER: 2010925186

McGraw-Hill books are available at special quantity discounts to use as premiums and sale promotions, or for use in corporate training programs. To contact a representative, please e-mail us at bulksales@mcgraw-hill.com.

Contents

How to Use This Book

This book is designed to help you build the skills you need to score well on the part of the ASVAB that is the most important—the AFQT or Armed Forces Qualifying Test. That test is the first hurdle you face in getting into the military. The AFQT is a subset of the ASVAB.

Your score on this test will make a huge difference in your military experience. First, if you don't score well enough, you won't be considered a viable candidate for enlistment. People with very low scores have no chance of getting into the military.

If you get a very low score, your ability to request a specific job and sign a contract for your preferred job is reduced. The higher your score, the more training and job options you will have. So why wouldn't you try to score the highest you can? A high score gives you much more control of your destiny in the U.S. Armed Forces.

The 50 skills in this book are the ones that are basic to doing well on the AFQT. They are the foundation skills for handling more complex issues and problems that you might encounter on the ASVAB and elsewhere. You can build on these skills to handle more demanding questions that you might find on the test.

To be clear, the test questions that you will encounter in this book are not the exact ones you will find on the AFQT. No book or online practice test has the exact questions that are on the AFQT. Be aware, too, that just taking a few free online tests is not enough to guarantee you a high AFQT score. It's much smarter to work though this book until you are competent in the 50 skills it teaches. You can then apply these skills to many of the AFQT items you will encounter.

A good way to start preparing for the AFQT is first to take the diagnostic pretest. That test will give you a good feel for the kinds of skills you need to succeed on the AFQT. After you complete the test, check the Scoring Sheet to see which answers you got wrong. That will help you to identify which of the 50 skills you should work on first. If you are hesitant about any of your answers, that should give you another indication of where you might be weak, and where you should focus your study time. The Pretest begins on page 13.

After you have identified your weakest skills, find the lessons in this book that are designed to strengthen those skills. Work your way through those lessons, then take the Posttest that begins on page 150. The results will help pinpoint where you have succeeded and where you still might want to review.

The 50 skills covered in this book tend to build on each other, so as you work through each lesson, look for any related skills listed at the bottom of the first page of each lesson. Reviewing the related skills can help you fully understand each skill that you study.

On the CD that accompanies this book, there are more practice items for you to take. Go ahead and take them to see how you do. Score each of the tests and review the skill explanations in the book for those items you answered incorrectly.

Use of this book will take you a long way toward a successful AFQT score for military entrance. Good luck in your military career!

What Is the ASVAB?

The Armed Services Vocational Aptitude Battery (ASVAB) is actually a group of individual aptitude tests. Each test measures something that is important for military entrance and/or for acceptance into training programs for certain military jobs. These tests are:

- **General Science** tests the ability to answer questions on a variety of science topics drawn from courses taught in most high schools. The life science items cover botany, zoology, anatomy and physiology, and ecology. The earth and space science items are based on astronomy, geology, meteorology, and oceanography. The physical science items measure force and motion mechanics, energy, fluids, atomic structure, and chemistry.

- **Arithmetic Reasoning** tests the ability to solve basic arithmetic problems one encounters in everyday life. One-step and multistep word problems require addition, subtraction, multiplication, and division, and choosing the correct order of operations when more than one step is necessary. The items include operations with whole numbers, operations with rational numbers, ratio and proportion, interest and percentage, and measurement. Arithmetic reasoning is one factor that helps characterize mathematics comprehension and logical thinking.

- **Word Knowledge** tests the ability to understand the meaning of words through synonyms—words having the same or nearly the same meaning as other words. The test is a measure of one component of reading comprehension since vocabulary is one of many factors that characterize reading comprehension.

- **Paragraph Comprehension** tests the ability to obtain information from written material. Students read different types of passages of varying lengths and respond to questions based on information presented in each passage. Concepts include identifying stated and reworded facts, determining a sequence of events, drawing conclusions, identifying main ideas, determining the author's purpose and tone, and identifying style and technique.

- **Mathematics Knowledge** tests the ability to solve problems by applying knowledge of mathematical concepts and applications. The problems focus on concepts and algorithms, and involve number theory, numeration, algebraic operations and equations, geometry and measurement, and probability. Mathematics knowledge is one factor that characterizes mathematics comprehension and assesses logical thinking.

- **Electronics Information** tests understanding of electrical current, circuits, devices, and systems. Topics include electrical circuits, electrical and electronic systems, electrical currents, electrical tools, symbols, devices, and materials.

- **Auto and Shop Information** tests aptitude for automotive maintenance and repair, and wood and metal shop practices. The test covers several areas commonly included in most high school auto and shop courses, such as automotive components, automotive systems, automotive tools, troubleshooting and repair, shop tools, building materials, and building and construction procedures.

- **Mechanical Comprehension** tests understanding of the principles of mechanical devices, structural support, and properties of materials. Mechanical comprehension topics include simple machines, compound machines, mechanical motion, and fluid dynamics.

Where Will You Take the ASVAB?

There are several places you might take the ASVAB test.

Your High School or Postsecondary School. Each year, thousands of students take the ASVAB at their school or one nearby. Your scores from this testing can be used for entrance into the military if you wish. If you think you can score higher, you will be able to take the test at a later point in time at another location. If you retake the ASVAB, this is the score that will count even if you scored higher on the high school test. So, be prepared to hone those skills if you take the test again.

At the high school, your test will be a paper-and-pencil version of the ASVAB. That means you will be in a room with a test administrator who reads the directions and times the test. You will be given a test booklet and an answer sheet. You will fill in the bubbles on the answer sheet and this will be scored. The results will be given to your school and possibly military recruiters.

There are several forms of the ASVAB test, so the version you will get is not likely to be the same as the one given to the person next to you.

Your Military Entrance Processing Station (MEPS). There are 65 MEPS. When you take the ASVAB at one of these locations, you will use the computer-adaptive version of the test. This version is called the CAT–ASVAB.

If you take this version of the test, you will be seated in front of a computer and monitor in a room with others. The test comes up on the screen. As you answer the test questions, the program records each answer, scores it, and then calculates your ability level. Based on that information, another item is selected. If you got the first answer wrong, the computer will give you an easier item. If you got it correct, the computer will give you a more difficult item. This process continues until you have completed the items provided to you. After you have completed the test, your Armed Forces Qualifying Test (AFQT—a subset of the ASVAB) score and other scores will be calculated.

You will also receive your physical exam at the MEPS and be sworn in there.

A Nearby Mobile Examination Team Site (MET). These 500 sites are in various locations across the country and are used if you are a significant distance away from a regular MEPS. Generally you will take the paper-and-pencil version of the ASVAB there to see if you are qualified on the Armed Forces Qualifying Test (AFQT). If you are, then you will go to a MEPS to continue your processing.

The U.S. Department of Defense has been testing an Internet version of the ASVAB, which should be similar to the computer adaptive version. At this writing it is unclear how widely this will be used in the near term. You may be among the first to take this Internet version.

Regular or Computer-Adaptive ASVAB: Does It Matter Which Version I Take?

Research shows that you will get the same score regardless of the version you take, so don't worry about that issue. Some individuals think the computerized version is harder, but that is because the questions are more closely aligned to your ability. In the paper-and-pencil version you will find questions that are very easy, medium difficult, and very difficult for you. You may feel better because you were able to answer the very easy questions, but your final score will be the same.

There are some possible advantages and disadvantages to each version, depending on your expectations.

Possible Advantages. One advantage of taking the CAT–ASVAB is that it takes less time than the paper-and-pencil version. Also, the test can be scored immediately, and scoring errors are reduced because of the automation. The test can be administered with minimal advance notice, whereas administration of the paper-and-pencil ASVAB needs to be scheduled well in advance. Unlike scores on the paper-and-pencil ASVAB, the CAT–ASVAB score you get is not based solely on the number of items you answered correctly. Some people have claimed that the CAT–ASVAB is easier and can give you better scores because you get more points for answering more difficult items.

Possible Disadvantages. Unlike the paper-and-pencil ASVAB, the CAT-ASVAB does not give you an opportunity to go back to questions you answered previously to change your answer or think about the question again. You also cannot skip questions and go on to other questions that you might know the answer to. If you get items wrong, the computer will give you easier items, but your score will be lower than if you correctly answered a few difficult items.

How Do You Position Yourself for the Best ASVAB/AFQT Outcome?

1. **Work through this book.** Be sure that you are competent in the skills that are listed. Each skill is briefly described and consists of examples and practice items. The answers for the practice items are given at the end of the book. You may also wish to spend time with other ASVAB books, such as *McGraw-Hill's ASVAB* and *McGraw-Hill's Basic Training for the AFQT*. Those books contain more instruction and practice for the math and verbal tests. *McGraw-Hill's ASVAB* also provides complete coverage of the other ASVAB subtests.
2. **Plan your study schedule in advance of your test session.** Instead of cramming the day before, spread your study out over several weeks or months prior to taking the ASVAB. In order to get the best score, be serious about your study. What you score on the ASVAB determines whether or not you get into the military and what kind of training and occupations you can enter.

3. **Start or keep a fitness program**. Move, participate in sports, lift weights, run, and walk. Obviously, this will help you do well on your physical exam and in basic training. If you have excess pounds, work them off. You will feel better, stronger, and smarter. You will have a more confident feeling. From the testing perspective though, the more physically fit you are, the more mentally fit you are. You will be able to learn things quicker, retain them longer, and think better on the day you test.

4. **Eat right**. You know what to do. Shed that fatty fast food diet that is loaded with bad fat and lots of calories. It gives you a bigger belly, makes you slower in your actions, and doesn't help your brain work better.

5. **Relax and sleep well**. Yes, you are a young energetic person and you think you can get by on lots of partying and minimal sleep. Your job here is to score well on the ASVAB, so you need to take every advantage you can. Getting a good night's sleep every night, but most importantly the night before your test, is critically important.

6. **Dump the stress**. Some level of stress is good as it keeps you on edge and thinking sharper, but excess stress is bad for your health and can be harmful to your thinking on test day.

The big day is finally here! You are ready for the ASVAB, and you are now at the MEPS. Here are some tips from recruiters to make the process go more smoothly.

1. Discuss any childhood medical problems with your parents and bring documentation with you.
2. Bring your Social Security card, birth certificate, and driver's license.
3. Remove all piercings.
4. Profanity and offensive wording or pictures on clothing are not tolerated.
5. Hats are not permitted inside the MEPS.
6. If you wear either eyeglasses or contacts, bring them along with your prescription and lens case.
7. Bathe or shower the night before your examination.
8. Wear underclothes.
9. Get a good night's sleep before taking the ASVAB.
10. Wear neat, moderate, comfortable clothing.
11. Don't bring stereo headphones, watches, jewelry, excessive cash, or any other valuables.
12. Ask your recruiter for a list of recommended personal items to bring to basic training.
13. Processing starts early at the MEPS—you must report on time.

What Is the ASVAB?

The Paper-and-Pencil ASVAB

Subtest	Minutes	Questions	Description
General Science	11	25	Measures knowledge of physical, earth and space, and biological sciences
Arithmetic Reasoning	36	30	Measures ability to solve basic arithmetic word problems
Word Knowledge	11	35	Measures ability to select the correct meaning of words presented through synonyms
Paragraph Comprehension	13	15	Measures ability to obtain information from written material
Mathematics Knowledge	24	25	Measures knowledge of high school mathematics concepts and applications
Electronics Information	9	20	Tests knowledge of electrical current, circuits, devices, and electronic systems
Auto and Shop Information	11	25	Measures knowledge of automotive maintenance and repair and wood and metal shop practices
Mechanical Comprehension	19	25	Measures knowledge of the principles of mechanical devices, structural support, and properties of materials

The CAT–ASVAB

Subtest	Minutes	Questions	Description
General Science	8	16	Measures knowledge of physical, earth and space, and biological sciences
Arithmetic Reasoning	39	16	Measures ability to solve basic arithmetic word problems
Word Knowledge	8	16	Measures ability to select the correct meaning of words presented through synonyms
Paragraph Comprehension	22	11	Measures ability to obtain information from written material
Mathematics Knowledge	18	16	Measures knowledge of high school mathematics concepts and applications
Electronics Information	8	16	Tests knowledge of electrical current, circuit, devices, and electronic systems
Auto Information	6	11	Measures knowledge of automotive maintenance and repair
Shop Information	5	11	Measures knowledge of wood and metal shop practices
Mechanical Comprehension	19	20	Measures knowledge of the principles of mechanical devices, structural support, and properties of materials
Assembling Objects	16	9	Measures the ability to interpret diagrams showing special relationships and how objects are related and connected

What Is the AFQT?

Four of the ASVAB tests are initially the most important for you. These are the two verbal tests (Word Knowledge and Paragraph Comprehension) and the two mathematics tests (Arithmetic Reasoning and Math Knowledge). These four tests make up what is called the Armed Forces Qualifying Test (AFQT). In order to even be considered for the military at all, you have to perform well on these four tests.

Your score on the AFQT is the sum of your scores on the two verbal (VE) tests and your scores on the Mathematics Knowledge (MK) and Arithmetic Reasoning (AR) tests. In math terms, the formula is $AFQT = 2VE + MK + AR$. That score is then compared to the scores of a nationally representative sample of other test takers aged 18 to 23 (the so-called "norm group") to produce a percentile score. The percentile indicates how well you ranked in comparison to the people in the norm group. Percentile scores run from 1–99. The higher the number, the better the score.

For example, if your AFQT score is 35, then you scored as well as or better than 35 percent of the people in the norm group. But that also means that 65 percent of the people in the norm group scored better than you did. You should aim for a much higher score!

The higher your score, the more attractive you are to the military because you will have shown a greater potential for success in a military career and in training programs. A high score demonstrates that you are ready and able to learn new material. The advantage for *you* in scoring well on the AFQT is that you will have many more jobs open to you. This means you have a greater selection of job and training opportunities. You will be in more control of your destiny in the military and beyond.

The military divides applicants into categories according to their AFQT scores. The categories are shown on the following chart.

Armed Forces Qualification Test (AFQT) Categories and Corresponding Percentile Percentile Score Ranges	
AFQT Category	**Percentile Score Range**
I	93–99
II	65–92
IIIA	50–64
IIIB	31–49
IV	10–30
V	1–9

The military is forbidden by law to enlist persons who earn an AFQT score in Category V. People with scores in Category IV generally do not get into the military because their scores are too low. On occasion in very difficult recruiting times, a few category IV people might get in if they meet other criteria such as having a high school diploma or some college credits. Category IIIB people are somewhat below average in trainability, but the military will enlist some individuals in this category for certain military occupations. The preference is for potential recruits to score at the 50th percentile or above, so that is the minimum you should aim for on the AFQT.

In addition to your scores on the AFQT, the military also prefers individuals who have completed high school and/or have some college credits. Why? Because it shows you have obtained some level of knowledge, are able to learn, and have the persistence to finish what you start!

The Armed Services are required to ensure that at least 90 percent of first-time recruits are high school graduates. Individual services often set even higher educational standards, sometimes requiring nearly 100 percent of the recruits in their enlistment pool to be high school graduates. If you don't have a high school diploma, you will need a very high AFQT score to be considered for the military.

Paying attention to the math and verbal skills in this book will help you reach the highest score you can.

Other Factors

There are several additional factors that are important in making you an attractive candidate: good moral character, decent financial character, good health, and a decent level of fitness. You should talk to a recruiter about these requirements and be sure to share any pertinent information about these areas.

To enter one of the services, you must meet rigorous moral character standards. This means no criminal record, no drugs, and the like. You will be screened by the recruiter and will undergo an interview covering your background. Be prepared to answer these questions clearly and honestly. A computerized search for a criminal record may be conducted, so your answers should match up to what the records show. Some types of criminal activity are clearly disqualifying; other cases require a waiver. The service to which you apply will examine your circumstances and make an individual determination of your qualifications.

You may undergo a financial credit check. Since it has been shown that applicants with existing financial problems generally do not overcome those problems on junior enlisted pay, your credit history may be part of the decision to allow you to enlist or not.

The day of enlistment you will undergo a physical exam. Be sure to bring your medical records and be prepared to answer questions about your health.

In addition to scoring high on the ASVAB, you need to be in reasonable physical shape. It may surprise you to learn that the #1 reason that young people are not eligible to enter the military is OBESITY! Staying in good physical condition will not only eliminate that obstacle, but your brain will also be in better shape to learn ASVAB skills and think through the answers to the test questions.

If You Are Serious about Enlisting

So, given all this information, what do you need to do to be eligible to enlist in one of the armed services? Here are seven pieces of advice. You should follow all of them.

1. Get good ASVAB scores. Study hard. The skills covered in this book will help you understand the kinds of skills that will be useful as you answer the test questions.
2. Reviewing you high school vocabulary and math skills will be especially useful to you, as those areas make up the AFQT.
3. Be sure you have a high school diploma.
4. Keep your weight in check. As you study for the test, take time to get in your exercise.
5. Stay off drugs—enough said.
6. Stay out of trouble. You are not attractive to the military services or society itself if you have a criminal record.
7. Keep your finances in shape. Don't get into debt. Manage your money smartly.

Types of AFQT Questions

The questions you'll encounter on the AFQT are generally fairly straightforward. Each one has four answer choices lettered A through D. Your job is to pick the correct choice. Here are some examples for each of the four AFQT tests.

Paragraph Comprehension

This test is to determine if you can understand what you read. You will be given a reading passage and then some questions to answer about the passage. Here are some sample questions to give you an idea of what to expect.

❶ From a building designer's standpoint, three things that make a home livable are the client, the building site, and the amount of money the client has to spend. According to this statement, to make a home livable,

Ⓐ the prospective piece of land makes little difference.

Ⓑ it can be built on any piece of land.

Ⓒ the design must fit the owner's income and site.

Ⓓ the design must fit the designer's income.

❷ Twenty-five percent of all household burglaries can be attributed to unlocked windows or doors. Crime is the result of opportunity plus desire. To prevent crime, it is each individual's responsibility to

Ⓐ provide the desire.

Ⓑ provide the opportunity.

Ⓒ prevent the desire.

Ⓓ prevent the opportunity.

❸ In certain areas, water is so scarce that every attempt is made to conserve it. For instance, on one oasis in the Sahara Desert the amount of water necessary for each date palm tree has been carefully determined. How much water should each tree be given?

Ⓐ No water at all

Ⓑ Exactly the amount required

Ⓒ Water on alternate days

Ⓓ Water only if it is healthy

❹ A thin transparent layer of oxide protects the metal titanium against corrosion. The same thin layer attracts artists interested in making their art with the help of technology. By using heat or electricity, an artist can thicken the oxide layer and thereby turn the metal a range of vivid colors.

According to the passage, some artists work with titanium because it

Ⓐ is transparent.

Ⓑ does not corrode.

Ⓒ generates its own heat.

Ⓓ can assume a variety of colors.

5 They returned to the beach, where blankets spotted the slope to the water. An advancing wall of clouds, black and gray, darkening the expanse of ground beneath, approached from the west. To the east and above them, the sky remained clear, the sun warm, as if collaborating in the deception.

The "deception" referred to in the passage is that

- Ⓐ there is no storm approaching.
- Ⓑ the sky is clear in the east.
- Ⓒ it is too cold to swim.
- Ⓓ the sun is warm.

Word Knowledge

This is basically a vocabulary test. Here are some examples.

1 *Small* most nearly means

- Ⓐ sturdy.
- Ⓑ round.
- Ⓒ cheap.
- Ⓓ little.

2 The wind is *variable* today.

- Ⓐ Mild
- Ⓑ Steady
- Ⓒ Shifting
- Ⓓ Chilling

3 *Rudiments* most nearly means

- Ⓐ politics.
- Ⓑ minute details.
- Ⓒ promotion opportunities.
- Ⓓ basic methods and procedures.

4 *Antagonize* most nearly means

- Ⓐ embarrass.
- Ⓑ struggle.
- Ⓒ provoke.
- Ⓓ worship.

5 His record provides no reason for *apprehension*.

- Ⓐ Anxiety
- Ⓑ Change
- Ⓒ Enjoyment
- Ⓓ Endorsement

Arithmetic Reasoning

1 If 12 workers are needed to run 4 machines, how many workers are needed to run 20 machines?

- Ⓐ 20
- Ⓑ 48
- Ⓒ 60
- Ⓓ 80

Types of AFQT Questions

❷ How many 36-passenger buses will it take to carry 144 people?

Ⓐ 3
Ⓑ 4
Ⓒ 5
Ⓓ 6

❸ If the tire of a car rotates at a constant speed of 552 times in one minute, how many times will the tire rotate in half an hour?

Ⓐ 276
Ⓑ 5,520
Ⓒ 8,280
Ⓓ 16,560

❹ A motorcycle costs $7,250. If it depreciates by 12% per year, how much will it be worth after one year?

Ⓐ $870
Ⓑ $1,250
Ⓒ $5,920
Ⓓ $6,380

❺ It costs $0.50 per square yard to waterproof canvas. What will it cost to waterproof a canvas truck cover that is 15′ × 24′?

Ⓐ $6.67
Ⓑ $18.00
Ⓒ $20.00
Ⓓ $180.00

Mathematics Knowledge

❶ If 50 percent of $X = 66$, then $X =$

Ⓐ 33
Ⓑ 66
Ⓒ 99
Ⓓ 132

❷ $\sqrt{\dfrac{23}{3}}$ is equal to

Ⓐ $\sqrt{3}$
Ⓑ 3
Ⓒ 9
Ⓓ 12

❸ If $X + 6 = 7$, then X is equal to

Ⓐ −1
Ⓑ 0
Ⓒ 1
Ⓓ $\dfrac{7}{6}$

4 What is the area of this square?

5 feet

Ⓐ 1 square foot

Ⓑ 5 square feet

Ⓒ 10 square feet

Ⓓ 25 square feet

5 $\dfrac{x^2 - y^2}{x - y}$ is equal to

Ⓐ $x + y$

Ⓑ $x - y$

Ⓒ $x + 2y$

Ⓓ $2x - y$

Now go on to the next chapter, the Pretest.

Taking the AFQT Pretest

This book covers 50 skills that you should have at the ready in order to perform well on the AFQT. The pretest in this chapter will help you identify which of these skills you need to work on in order to get a better score.

DIRECTIONS: Take the pretest. Give yourself 45 minutes to complete this test. If you take more than 45 minutes, then you need to work hard on your skills and your concentration.

For each question on this the pretest, circle the letter of your answer choice. When you are finished, turn to the Scoring Sheet on page 24. Write down your answer to each question in the space provided. Then see if you got the answer right or wrong. If you got the answer wrong, you definitely need to review the pages in the book that relate to that skill. Each item tracks with one of the 50 skills. So if you got Item 3 wrong, you need to go to the skill listed and review it to be sure you understand the concept. There are 22 reading skills and 28 math skills. The skills are laser-focused on helping you get a high AFQT score because that is your major hurdle to getting accepted into the military.

Even for test items that you get correct, it will do you good to go to the corresponding skill pages and review and practice the example items.

Here is an example of how you should think about your score and answers. The following sample scoring sheet shows that the test-taker answered Items 1, 2, 5, 6, 10 and 11 correctly. However, he or she answered Items 3, 4, 7, 8, and 9 incorrectly. As you can see in the column labeled "Skill #," these incorrect items relate to Skills 3, 4, 13, 9, and 6. These numbered skills are the ones covered in this book. For example, Skill 3 is covered on page 30, and Skill 13 is covered on page 50. These are the skills that this test-taker should tackle first.

Item	Skill #	Pages in Book	Your Answer	Correct Answer	Were you correct? Y or N
1	1		B	B	Y
2	2		D	D	Y
3	3		A	D	N
4	4		B	A	N
5	5		C	C	Y
6	8		A	A	Y
7	13		C	B	N
8	9		B	C	N
9	6		B	A	N
10	7		D	D	Y
11	10		C	C	Y

You MUST review these skills. You need to go to the pages listed to review the skills.

You MUST review these skills. You need to go to the pages listed to review the skills.

AFQT Pretest

The following 50 questions represent the 50 skills covered in this book. The first 22 questions check your reading, and the remaining 28 check your math knowledge.

For each question, circle the answer of your choice. At the end of the test, transfer your answers to the Scoring Sheet on page 24 to check your work.

Questions 1–8 are based on the following reading passage.

Parents are key influencers of physical activity in their children. Building moderate-intensity physical activity into the daily routine may help parents model this desirable behavior for their children. **(1)** Reducing the time spent in parental sedentary behaviors, such as television watching or computer use, may serve as a model for children to use time appropriately.

Serving as a role model for children is a further reason for adults to engage in regular physical activity, in addition to its contribution to one's own health, sense of well-being, and maintenance of a healthy body weight. In contrast, sedentary lifestyles are associated with increased risk for overweight and obesity and many chronic diseases. **(2)** For these reasons, the *2005 Dietary Guidelines for Americans* recommend that individuals engage in regular physical activity and reduce sedentary activities.

In a scientific study, it was discovered that about three-quarters (73.8 percent) of adults (ages 19 and older) reported that they had not walked or bicycled to work or school or to do errands in the past 30 days. Of the one-quarter (26.2 percent) who had commuted via walking or biking, most (21.9 percent) did so at least once a week, on average (>4 times a month). However, only about one in ten (9.6 percent of all adults) did so five or more times per week (>20 times a month).

While about 70 percent of all adults reported that, at some point in the last 30 days, they had engaged in moderate or higher intensity household tasks for at least 10 minutes, most did so twice a week or less. The median number of times reported was six per month. **(3)** Three-quarters of all adults reported doing at least 10 minutes of these physically active household chores less than three times per week (<13 times per month), and only 10 percent reported doing these chores daily (>30 times per month).

A much larger percentage of adults reported that they spent time in sedentary behaviors on a daily basis. About two-thirds of all adults (67.5 percent) reported watching TV or videos an average of 2 hours or more per day in the past 30 days. In addition, a quarter of adults (25.2 percent) used a computer outside of work or played computer games an average of 2 hours or more per day. **(4)** They spent 2 or more hours per day watching television or videos, and reported using a computer outside of work for 2 or more hours a day. The majority of adults reported an average of 2 or more hours per day sitting and watching television.

1. Which of the numbered sentences in the paragraph is the best representation of the main idea?

   Ⓐ 1
   Ⓑ 2
   Ⓒ 3
   Ⓓ 4

2. Which of the following is the best summary statement or main idea of the passage?

   Ⓐ Too many adults spend their time on the computer or watching TV.
   Ⓑ Most adults do at least 10 minutes of exercise every day.
   Ⓒ Parents should be examples to their children and exercise more.
   Ⓓ Parents should encourage their children to get physical activity through household chores.

3. Of the following, which is the best title for this passage?

   Ⓐ Adults Should Be Role Models for Their Children
   Ⓑ Better Health Through Exercise
   Ⓒ Pay Attention to Scientific Studies
   Ⓓ Stop Watching TV and Playing on Computers: It's Not Good for You

4. What percentage of adults reported watching TV or videos an average of 2 hours or more per day in the past 30 days?

   Ⓐ 25.2
   Ⓑ 27.2
   Ⓒ 67.5
   Ⓓ 70.0

5. What conclusion can you draw from this passage?

   Ⓐ Children need a lot more exercise.
   Ⓑ Young people need to spend less time watching TV and on the computer.
   Ⓒ Parents need to increase the amount of exercise that they get each day.
   Ⓓ Parents need to understand that they are role models for their children.

6. What is the major purpose of the author in this passage?

   Ⓐ Inform
   Ⓑ Entertain
   Ⓒ Create fear
   Ⓓ Offer an opinion

7. What is the meaning of *sedentary* in this passage?

   Ⓐ Active
   Ⓑ Inactive
   Ⓒ Exhilarating
   Ⓓ Cautious

8. Look at the sentence labeled (1). Does this sentence represent fact or opinion?

   Ⓐ Fact
   Ⓑ Opinion

Questions 9–11 are based on the following passage.

When the power goes out, here's what you should do to keep your food safe. Your health and safety depend on you following these suggestions. People have been known to go into a coma and never recover because they didn't understand how serious this situation really is.

First and foremost, keep the refrigerator and freezer doors closed as much as possible to maintain the cold temperature. The refrigerator will keep food cold for about 4 hours if it is unopened.

Second, if you plan to eat refrigerated or frozen meat, eggs, poultry, or fish while it is still at safe temperatures, it's important that each item is thoroughly cooked to the proper temperature to assure that any foodborne bacteria that may be present are destroyed.

Third, if at any point the food was above 40 °F for 2 hours or more—discard it. You can be in serious danger of becoming very ill if you don't follow these suggestions.

9 What kind of mood is the author trying to convey in this passage?

Ⓐ Concerned

Ⓑ Fanciful

Ⓒ Funny

Ⓓ Sympathetic

10 According to the passage, what is the first thing you should do to preserve food in a refrigerator when the power goes out?

Ⓐ Cook the food.

Ⓑ Keep the refrigerator door shut.

Ⓒ Keep the food at freezing temperature.

Ⓓ Discard most of the food.

11 Which of the following is the best summary statement or paraphrase of the passage?

Ⓐ There are several actions you can take to keep your food safe when the power goes out. Keep your refrigerator door shut, cook your food thoroughly, and discard any item you think might be a potential hazard.

Ⓑ When the power goes out, keep your food below 40 degrees so that you are not in danger of eating spoiled food.

Ⓒ Be sure that your refrigerator is able to keep food at a temperature where you are not likely to eat food that is spoiled. This is especially important when the power goes out.

Ⓓ Be sure to cook your food before eating when the power goes out, otherwise throw it away. If you don't, there could be dire outcomes.

AFQT Pretest

Questions 12–13 are based on the following passage.

The government of the United States is made up of three branches: the Legislative Branch, the Executive Branch, and the Judicial Branch. The Legislative Branch, called Congress, is responsible for making laws. Congress is made up of two houses: the Senate and the House of Representatives.

There are many differences between the Senate and the House of Representatives. The Vice President of the United States is the head of the Senate. He must vote in the Senate if there is a tie. The leader of the House of Representatives is called the Speaker of the House. The representatives elect him or her. Another difference is that the Senate is made up of 100 senators, two from each state.

The House of Representatives is made up of 435 representatives. The number of representatives from each state is determined by that state's population. The greater the population in a state, the more representatives that state has in the House.

A third difference is that senators are elected to 6-year terms, while representatives are elected to serve 2-year terms. Every 2 years, the nation holds an election for members of Congress.

Before the President can sign a bill into law, it must first be approved by a majority of members in both the House and Senate.

12. Which part of the Legislative Branch best represents the actual population of the states?
- Ⓐ House
- Ⓑ Congress
- Ⓒ Senate
- Ⓓ Speaker

13. Which of the following can you infer from this passage?
- Ⓐ The Vice President is the most powerful member of Congress.
- Ⓑ In the Senate, a large state like Texas has the same representation as a small state like New Hampshire.
- Ⓒ The Speaker of the House represents the entire country.
- Ⓓ All of the above.

14. In the word *carnivorous*, the root word means
- Ⓐ Meat
- Ⓑ East
- Ⓒ Street
- Ⓓ Corner

15. The prefix *circum-* means
- Ⓐ Around
- Ⓑ Between
- Ⓒ Before
- Ⓓ Lastly

16. The suffix *-ectomy* means
- Ⓐ First
- Ⓑ Lastly
- Ⓒ Combine
- Ⓓ Cutting

⑰ The word that most nearly means *implausible* is

Ⓐ Unbelievable

Ⓑ Superior

Ⓒ Significant

Ⓓ Cooperative

⑱ The word that most nearly means *abstemious* is

Ⓐ Incredible

Ⓑ Self-denying

Ⓒ Self-sacrificing

Ⓓ Obstinate

⑲ The meaning of *coalesce* is

Ⓐ Battle with your neighbors

Ⓑ A lively part

Ⓒ Come together

Ⓓ Set yourself apart

⑳ Which is the correct word to use in the following sentence?

Because she was trying to be in control, she would *medal/meddle* in the affairs of others.

Ⓐ Medal

Ⓑ Meddle

㉑ Which of the following is the antonym of *affluent*?

Ⓐ Applicant

Ⓑ Comfortable

Ⓒ Portion

Ⓓ Poor

㉒ Which is the correct usage in this sentence?

The tourist wrote a letter to her friend on the hotel *stationary/stationery*.

Ⓐ Stationary

Ⓑ Stationery

AFQT Pretest

Questions 23–50 are math questions.

23 Add the following numbers.

    1,569
    6,709
    4,409
  + 5,607

Ⓐ 27,294

Ⓑ 18,294

Ⓒ 19,284

Ⓓ 19,584

24 Multiply the following numbers.

    679,987
    × 569

Ⓐ 386,942,603

Ⓑ 386,912,703

Ⓒ 386,912,603

Ⓓ 389,912,603

25 Divide the following numbers.

560,148 ÷ 46,679 =

Ⓐ 12

Ⓑ 13

Ⓒ 14

Ⓓ 15

26 Add the following numbers.

  − 987
  + 345

Ⓐ − 542

Ⓑ − 652

Ⓒ + 642

Ⓓ − 642

27 Round this number to the nearest thousand.

9,856,867.9689

Ⓐ 9,857,000

Ⓑ 8,860,000

Ⓒ 985,867

Ⓓ 9,856,867.969

28 Solve the following problem.

$(10 \times 10) + 2^2 + (-9 \times -9)(2) =$

Ⓐ 58

Ⓑ 266

Ⓒ 264

Ⓓ 79

29 Change the following fraction into a decimal.

$$\frac{894}{2,473} =$$

Ⓐ 0.456

Ⓑ 0.782

Ⓒ 0.362

Ⓓ 0.258

AFQT Pretest

30 Which of the following is $\frac{36}{7}$ written as a decimal rounded to the nearest hundredth?

  Ⓐ 5.26
  Ⓑ 5.14
  Ⓒ 6.14
  Ⓓ 6.26

31 Solve the following problem.

$$17\frac{3}{4}$$
$$-18\frac{2}{3}$$

  Ⓐ $1\frac{1}{3}$
  Ⓑ $35-\frac{1}{1}$
  Ⓒ $35\frac{5}{12}$
  Ⓓ $-\frac{11}{12}$

32 What is the answer to the following problem?

$$6\frac{3}{5} \div 2\frac{1}{5} =$$

  Ⓐ $\frac{33}{5}$
  Ⓑ $\frac{165}{5}$
  Ⓒ $\frac{33}{11}$
  Ⓓ 3

33 What is the decimal equivalent of 97%?

  Ⓐ 0.97
  Ⓑ 0.09
  Ⓒ 0.097
  Ⓓ 0.0097

34 Which of the following is the equivalent of 4^{-3}?

  Ⓐ 64
  Ⓑ $\frac{3}{4}$
  Ⓒ $\frac{1}{64}$
  Ⓓ −12

35 What is the answer to the following problem?

$(2.45 \times 10^5)(3.61 \times 10^{-3}) =$

  Ⓐ 8.8445×10^8
  Ⓑ 8.8445×10^2
  Ⓒ 8.8445×10^{-3}
  Ⓓ 8.8445×10^{-2}

36 Calculate the mean of the following numbers.

37, 56, 57, 78, 89, 112, 34, 17, 99, 221, 234

  Ⓐ 76
  Ⓑ 89
  Ⓒ 94
  Ⓓ 99

37. The following graph shows the total average snowfall per state over the course of one year for several states. Which two states have a total snowfall of 496.2 inches?

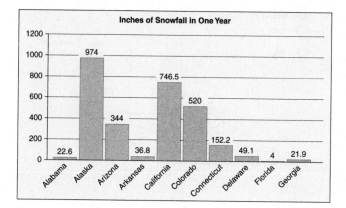

Inches of Snowfall in One Year

Ⓐ Alabama and California
Ⓑ Arizona and Delaware
Ⓒ Colorado and Connecticut
Ⓓ Arizona and Connecticut

38. What are the factors of $y^2 + 16y + 28$?

Ⓐ $(y + 28)y$
Ⓑ $(y + 14)(y + 2)$
Ⓒ $(y + 7)(y - 3)$
Ⓓ $y^2(y + 12)$

39. Gary puts $15,000 in an account that earns 4% annual interest for 2 years. How much money will he have at the end of that time?

Ⓐ $16,200
Ⓑ $16,400
Ⓒ $16,000
Ⓓ $16,800

40. If a bricklayer can lay 175 bricks per hour, how many bricks can he lay in an 8-hour day?

Ⓐ 1000
Ⓑ 1350
Ⓒ 1400
Ⓓ 1750

41. Clint has a racecar that goes 137 miles per hour. If he can keep up that pace for 6.5 hours, how far will he go?

Ⓐ 450.5 miles
Ⓑ 545.0 miles
Ⓒ 667.5 miles
Ⓓ 890.5 miles

42. A TV infomercial says that if you purchase a certain CD collection within the next 30 minutes, you can get the entire collection for $110. The original price was $280. What percent will you save if you make the purchase now?

Ⓐ 47%
Ⓑ 52%
Ⓒ 61%
Ⓓ 71%

43. Dakota has a jar full of coins. There are 512 pennies, 430 nickels, 520 dimes, 623 quarters, and 30 half dollars. If every coin has an equal chance of being pulled, what is the probability that the first coin Dakota pulls from the jar will be a dime?

Ⓐ 10%
Ⓑ 25%
Ⓒ 35%
Ⓓ 52%

44 In the figure below, if angle *CBD* measures 82°, what is the measure of angle *ABC*?

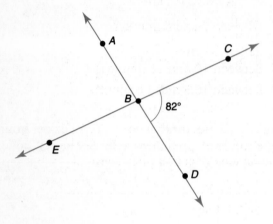

Ⓐ 82°
Ⓑ 87°
Ⓒ 92°
Ⓓ 98°

45 In the right triangle below, if side *a* measures 9.1 inches and side *b* measures 14.7 inches, about how long is side *c*?

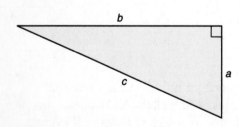

Ⓐ 12.25 inches
Ⓑ 15.35 inches
Ⓒ 16.76 inches
Ⓓ 17.29 inches

46 In the rhombus below, if angle *ABC* measures 150°, and line *AC* bisects angle *BCD*, what is the measure of angle *BCA*?

Ⓐ 15°
Ⓑ 25°
Ⓒ 55°
Ⓓ 75°

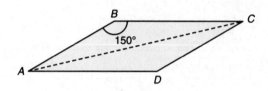

47 Danny is creating a patio that has 5 sides. The sides measure 3 yards, 5 yards, 6 feet, 8 feet, and 12 feet. What is the perimeter of the patio?

Ⓐ 34 yards
Ⓑ 54 yards
Ⓒ 50 feet
Ⓓ 74 feet

48 Garth and Gabby are planning to build a tiled patio. If the patio is a square with a side of 10 feet and the tiles are squares of 12 inches, how many tiles will they need to use?

Ⓐ 50 tiles
Ⓑ 100 tiles
Ⓒ 144 tiles
Ⓓ 200 tiles

㊾ Harley is filling his swimming pool with water. The pool is 17 feet long, 9 feet wide, and 8 feet deep. If his hose is able to fill the pool at a rate of 48 cubic feet per hour, how many hours will it take to fill the pool?

Ⓐ 12 hours

Ⓑ 25.5 hours

Ⓒ 34.4 hours

Ⓓ 36.9 hours

㊿ An exercise ball has a diameter of 3 feet. If a pump can push in air at a rate of 2 cubic feet per minute, about how long will it take to inflate the exercise ball?

Ⓐ Between 7 and 8 minutes

Ⓑ Between 8 and 9 minutes

Ⓒ Between 10 and 11 minutes

Ⓓ Between 10.5 and 11 minutes

STOP. This is the end of the AFQT Pretest. Use the Scoring Sheet on page 24 to check your answers.

AFQT Pretest

Scoring Your Answers

Write your answers on this scoring sheet in the 4th column. Compare your answers to the correct answers in the 5th column. In the last column, indicate if you answered correctly or not. Where you got an answer wrong, circle the skill and the page number in this book where the skill is reviewed and explained.

Now start working through the lessons for each of those skills found throughout the remainder of this book.

Pretest Scoring Sheet					
Item	**Skill #**	**Book Pages**	**Your Answer**	**Correct Answer**	**Correct Y or N**
1	1	26–27		A	
2	2	28–29		C	
3	3	30–31		A	
4	4	32–33		C	
5	5	34–35		D	
6	8	40–41		A	
7	13	50–51		B	
8	9	42–43		A	
9	6	36–37		A	
10	7	38–39		B	
11	10	44–45		A	
12	11	46–47		A	
13	12	48–49		B	
14	14	52–53		A	
15	15	54–57		A	
16	16	58–61		D	
17	17	62–65		A	
18	18	66–69		B	
19	19	70–73		C	
20	20	74–77		B	
21	21	78–79		D	
22	22	80–81		B	
23	23	82–83		B	
24	24	84–85		C	
25	25	86–87		A	

(Continued)

Item	Skill #	Book Pages	Your Answer	Correct Answer	Correct Y or N
26	26	88–89		D	
27	27	90–91		A	
28	28	92–93		B	
29	29	94–95		C	
30	30	96–97		B	
31	31	98–99		D	
32	32	100–101		D	
33	33	102–103		A	
34	34	104–105		C	
35	35	106–107		B	
36	36	108–109		C	
37	37	110–113		D	
38	38	114–117		B	
39	39	118–119		A	
40	40	120–121		C	
41	41	122–123		D	
42	42	124–125		C	
43	43	126–127		B	
44	44	128–131		D	
45	45	132–135		D	
46	46	136–139		A	
47	47	140–141		C	
48	48	142–145		B	
49	49	146–147		B	
50	50	148–149		A	

Pretest Scoring Sheet (Cont.)

Find the Main Idea in a Sentence in the Passage

On the ASVAB you might be asked to identify the main idea of a paragraph. The main idea is the thought or set of words that best describes the meaning of the paragraph. It's the main message that the author wants to convey. As you read a paragraph, your goal is to decide what the paragraph is generally about—to identify the main idea.

Often the author will state the main idea in the first sentence and then provide supporting ideas and facts later in the passage. So when you are looking for the main idea of a passage, be sure to look closely at the first sentence. However, sometimes an author will provide the supporting information first, and then end with a sentence that gives the main idea. Other times you will find the main idea elsewhere in the passage.

Example
Read the paragraph and answer the question.

① If you want to get rid of your old computer, options include recycling, reselling, and donating. ② But before you log off for the last time, there are important things to do to prepare it for disposal. ③ Computers often hold personal and financial information, including passwords, account numbers, license keys or registration numbers for software programs, addresses and phone numbers, medical and prescription information, tax returns, and other personal documents that you might not want others to see. ④ Before getting rid of your old computer, it's a good idea to use software to "wipe" the hard drive clean.

Of the following which sentence best reflects the main idea of the paragraph?

Ⓐ 1
Ⓑ 2
Ⓒ 3
Ⓓ 4

Solution: It's easy to be fooled into thinking that the first sentence is the main idea because it lists various ways that you can dispose of a computer. But this is a case in which the main idea is not in the first sentence of the paragraph. The main point of this paragraph is to warn you that your computer can hold personal information that you might not want others to see. Then there are smaller, supporting ideas about wiping the hard drive clean, logging off for the last time, and recycling and donating your computer; but these are secondary to the main idea.

Find the Main Idea in a Sentence in the Passage

Test Yourself!

Read the following paragraph and answer the question. Circle the letter of your choice.

① Increased intake of fruits, vegetables, whole grains, and fat-free or low-fat milk and milk products are likely to have important health benefits for most Americans. ② While protein is an important nutrient in the diet, most Americans are already currently consuming enough and do not need to increase their intake. ③ Associations have been identified between specific food groups (like fruits and vegetables) and reduced risk for chronic diseases. ④ The strength of the evidence for the association between increased intake of fruits and vegetables and reduced risk of chronic diseases is variable and depends on the specific disease, but an array of evidence points to beneficial health effects.

Which sentence in the paragraph best represents the main idea?

Ⓐ 1
Ⓑ 2
Ⓒ 3
Ⓓ 4

Read the following paragraph and answer the question. Circle the letter of your choice.

① As students use primary sources, they begin to view their textbook as only one interpretation, and its author as an interpreter of evidence, not as a messenger of truth. ② For example, as students read personal letters from distressed farmers to President Franklin D. Roosevelt, look at reports on economic conditions across America, or listen to recordings of government-produced radio dramas, they compare the importance of these sources against such generalizations as found in their textbook. For instance, author Miles Simpson states, "The most urgent task that Roosevelt faced when he took office was to provide food, clothing, and shelter for millions of jobless, hungry, cold, despairing Americans." ③ Students begin to understand that such generalizations are interpretations of past events, but not the only interpretation. ④ They become aware that the text has a point of view that does not make it incorrect, but does render it subject to question. ⑤ Primary sources force students to realize that any account of an event, no matter how impartially presented it appears to be, is essentially subjective.

Which sentence in the paragraph best represents the main idea?

Ⓐ 1
Ⓑ 2
Ⓒ 3
Ⓓ 4
Ⓔ 5

Choose the Best Summary Statement of the Main Idea

In the previous skill, you saw that on the ASVAB or other tests you may be asked to identify which sentence in a reading passage best reflects the main idea of that passage. But sometimes on tests you might be asked to think about the total "big picture" idea that is being conveyed, and then select a sentence from several choices that best conveys that main idea. None of the choices will be a sentence from the original passage.

Let's look at the same paragraph we studied in the previous skill. On the ASVAB, you might get a question that is phrased as shown below.

Read the paragraph and answer the question.

> If you want to get rid of your old computer, options include recycling, reselling, and donating. But before you log off for the last time, there are important things to do to prepare it for disposal. Computers often hold personal and financial information, including passwords, account numbers, license keys or registration numbers for software programs, addresses and phone numbers, medical and prescription information, tax returns, and other personal documents that you might not want others to see. Before getting rid of your old computer, it's a good idea to use software to "wipe" the hard drive clean.
>
> Which of the following sentences best reflects the main idea of the paragraph?
>
> Ⓐ Computers should be recycled or donated to others because this is best for the environment.
> Ⓑ Remove personal information before donating your computer.
> Ⓒ Wipe the hard drive clean before logging off your computer.
> Ⓓ Make sure you don't keep medical information on your computer system.

In this situation, you are not asked which sentence in the passage best represents the main idea, but rather which sentence in the answer choices best reflects the main idea.

Choice B is the best answer because it best reflects the central message of the paragraph, which is that you should eliminate any personal information from your computer before getting rid of it. The other answer choice sentences merely convey other information that can be related to this main idea. None of them fully covers the most important point that the author is trying to convey.

Remember that with this type of question, your goal is to select the answer choice that fully reflects the main idea that the author is trying to communicate to the reader.

Choose the Best Summary Statement of the Main Idea

Test Yourself!

Read the paragraph and answer the question. Circle the letter of your choice.

The World Digital Library offers free online access to important, rare, and interesting cultural treasures from around the planet. The vast collection of manuscripts, maps, rare books, sound recordings, films, prints, photographs, and other cultural and historical materials can be viewed with the click of a computer mouse. The site is in seven major languages, permitting users to conduct searches and read descriptions of the content in Arabic, Chinese, English, French, Russian, Spanish, and Portuguese. All materials are presented in their original languages. For selected items, there are videos featuring discussions by expert curators. This is only the beginning of an ambitious project to share the contents of the world's libraries and cultural institutions.

Which of the following sentences best reflects the main idea of the paragraph?

Ⓐ Libraries have materials in many languages.
Ⓑ The World Digital Library provides materials in their original languages.
Ⓒ Making the World Digital Library is a huge project of vast importance.
Ⓓ The World Digital Library provides a vast array of documents via computer.

Read the paragraph and answer the question. Circle the letter of your choice.

Acid rain is becoming more prevalent in this country and across the globe. It looks, feels, and tastes just like clean rain. The harm to people from acid rain is not direct. Walking in acid rain, or even swimming in an acid lake, is no more dangerous than walking or swimming in clean water. However, the pollutants that cause acid rain—sulfur dioxide (SO_2) and nitrogen oxides (NO_x)—do damage human health. These gases interact in the atmosphere to form fine particles that can be transported long distances by winds and inhaled deep into people's lungs. Fine particles can also penetrate indoors. Many scientific studies have identified a relationship between high levels of fine particles and increased illness and premature death from heart and lung disorders.

Which of the following sentences best reflects the main idea of the paragraph?

Ⓐ Acid rain can be harmless even if you walk or swim in it because it is the same as regular rain.
Ⓑ The fine particles in acid rain can be carried great distances and be transported to any part of the country
Ⓒ People die because of acid rain.
Ⓓ Acid rain can harm humans because of the fine particles that are breathed in by people.

Read the paragraph and answer the question.

A northeaster is a winter storm that forms in the mid-latitudes between the months of September and April. Although northeasters are generally not as intense as hurricanes, their slow movement can cause damage to large areas of the coastline. One of the most destructive storms ever experienced in the Mid-Atlantic States was the Ash Wednesday storm of 1962. With wind speeds measured at 60 mph, this storm lasted five tidal cycles, causing damage to more than 600 miles of shoreline. The infamous "Perfect Storm," also known as the 1991 Halloween Northeaster, was a strong northeaster fueled by Hurricane Grace and the Gulf Stream current. Storm winds eventually reached 69 mph, causing $1 billion in damage along the northeastern United States and Canadian coastlines.

Which of the following represents the best summary of the main idea of the passage?

Ⓐ Northeaster storms are more devastating than hurricanes.
Ⓑ Northeaster storms are very dangerous and destructive.
Ⓒ The Gulf Stream helps create northeaster storms.
Ⓓ The northeaster storm of 1962 was the worst ever experienced.

Identify the Best Title

Another way to identify the main idea of a reading passage and to show that you understand what you are reading is to think about the best title for that passage. The best title would be a word or phrase that describes the entire passage, not just a part of it.

Let's read a passage and think through the best title for it. Remember that the best title should be something that ties the entire passage together in the best way.

> Three athletes are highlighted in the summer issue of *Sports Illustrated* magazine. Here is some general information on each one. Starting on page 26 you can find in-depth stories on each athlete by our own editor, Max Persell.
>
> Oscar De La Hoya, nicknamed the Golden Boy, is a Mexican-American boxer who defeated 17 world champions and won 10 world titles. In 1992, he won a gold medal in boxing at the Barcelona Olympic Games. Outside the boxing ring, he has released a Grammy-nominated Latin pop album and started a charitable foundation to help educate underprivileged youth.
>
> Celebrated Puerto Rican right fielder Roberto Clemente started the trend of Hispanic players excelling in U.S. Major League Baseball. He was drafted by the Pittsburgh Pirates in 1954 and played 18 seasons for them. He won 12 Golden Glove awards for his fielding prowess and was named the National League's Most Valuable Player (1966) and World Series MVP (1971). Clemente died in 1972 when a plane he was on that was delivering humanitarian supplies to earthquake victims.
>
> In 2003, Mexican–American football (soccer) player Carlos Bocanegra became the first U.S. defender since 1994 to score four goals in one year. Born in California, Bocanegra was drafted by U.S. Major League Soccer's Chicago Fire in 2000. He was Rookie of the Year in 2000 and was named MLS Defender of the Year in 2002 and 2003 before transferring to England's Fulham Football Club. In 2008, he signed with the Rennes, France, football club.

Of the following, which is the best title for this passage?

Ⓐ Soccer, Baseball, and Boxing
Ⓑ Sports in a Minute
Ⓒ Hispanic Athletes
Ⓓ Winning Teams

Choice A: Although the passage does talk about a soccer player, a baseball player, and a boxer, these three sports are not a unifying theme for all of the paragraphs.

Choice B: There is nothing in the reading passage to give you the idea that the passage relates to a particular minute of time. Also, the passage does not cover many sports, just three specific ones.

Choice D: The passage certainly has something to do with winning athletes, but not necessarily teams. For example, Oscar De La Hoya, a boxer, is not a member of a team.

Choice C: This is the best answer because the entire passage is about athletes who are Hispanic.

Identify the Best Title

Test Yourself!

❶ Can you think of other possible titles for the passage you just read? List them in the spaces below.

_____

_____

Let's try another passage.

❷ *Read the passage and answer the question.*

"The Star-Spangled Banner" (written in 1814 by lawyer/poet Francis Scott Key and declared the national anthem in 1931) is invariably played on Independence Day. The song's rousing refrain recalls the early struggles of a nation. Less than two decades after the debut of "The Star-Spangled Banner," the Reverend Samuel Francis Smith wrote the lyrics to "My Country, 'Tis of Thee'" (adapted from the British national anthem "God Save the Queen"), which became a patriotic staple.

In the late 19th century, classics of the Civil War era were added to the national repertoire, notably "Battle Cry of Freedom" and "Battle Hymn of the Republic."

"America the Beautiful" appeared as a poem in 1895, written by Katharine Lee Bates, a professor at Wellesley College. In the early 1900s, it was set to music by Samuel A. Ward and achieved national popularity.

List some possible titles for this passage.

_____

_____

Focus on Facts and Details

On the ASVAB, you will be asked to find factual details in reading passages. Your best bet for these questions is first to read the question to see what fact or detail is required, and then to read the paragraph to find the answer to the question. You can look for key words mentioned in the question as you read the passage. Be sure to read the entire passage. Don't just look for the specific answer. All of the facts mentioned in the answer choices may be present in the passage, but only one will be the correct answer to the question.

As you read the passage, put your finger on the section that probably gives the answer to the question, so that you can find it again. Then after you have read the question again, go back to the part of the passage that you "fingered" as the place that has the answer so that you can double-check it.

Here is an example. Read the following paragraph and answer the questions.

Compared with the many people who consume a diet with only small amounts of fruits and vegetables, those who eat more generous amounts as part of a healthful diet are likely to have reduced risk of chronic diseases, including stroke and other cardiovascular diseases, type 2 diabetes, and cancers in certain sites (oral cavity and pharynx, larynx, lung, esophagus, stomach, and colon-rectum). Diets rich in foods containing fiber, such as fruits, vegetables, and whole grains, may reduce the risk of coronary heart disease. Diets rich in milk and milk products can reduce the risk of low bone mass throughout the life cycle. The consumption of milk products is especially important for children and adolescents who are building their peak bone mass and developing lifelong habits. Although each of these food groups may have a different relationship with disease outcomes, the adequate consumption of all food groups contributes to overall health.

According to the passage, which foods may reduce coronary heart disease?

Ⓐ Fiber and whole grains
Ⓑ Milk and fruits
Ⓒ Vegetables and meats
Ⓓ Potatoes and sugars

By reading the question first, you know that you should be looking for a mention of coronary heart disease. You'll find coronary heart disease mentioned in the middle of the passage in the sentence, "Diets rich in foods containing fiber, such as fruits, vegetables, and whole grains, may reduce the risk of coronary heart disease." The sentence clearly states that fiber and whole grains are related to a reduced risk in coronary heart disease. Choice A is the correct answer.

Focus on Facts and Details

Test Yourself!

For the same passage, try this question. Circle the letter of your choice.

1 According to the passage, why is drinking milk important for young people?

- (A) It prevents cancer.
- (B) It prevents diabetes.
- (C) It is difficult to obtain as an adult.
- (D) It helps build bone mass.

Read the following passage and answer the questions. For each question, circle the letter of your choice.

For the first time, NASA's Hubble Space Telescope has seen distinctly the "tenth planet," currently nicknamed "Xena," and found that it's only slightly larger than Pluto.

Though previous ground-based observations suggested that Xena's diameter was about 30 percent greater than Pluto, Hubble observations, taken Dec. 9 and 10, 2005, showed Xena's diameter as 1,490 miles. Pluto's diameter, as measured by Hubble, is 1,422 miles.

Only a handful of images were required to determine Xena's diameter. Located 10 billion miles from Earth with a diameter a little more than half the width of the United States, the object is 1.5 pixels across in Hubble's view. That's enough to make a precise size measurement.

Because Xena is smaller than previously thought, but comparatively bright, it must be one of the most reflective objects in the solar system. The only object more reflective is Enceladus, a geologically active moon of Saturn whose surface is continuously recoated with highly reflective ice by active geysers.

2 According to the passage, which is the object that is brighter than Xena?

- (A) Hubble
- (B) Pluto
- (C) Earth
- (D) Enceladus

3 According to the passage, how far away is Xena from Earth?

- (A) 10 billion miles
- (B) 1.5 pixels
- (C) 1,422 miles
- (D) 1,490 miles

Read the following passage and answer the question. Circle the letter of your choice.

Six major groups make up the Brazilian population: the Portuguese, who colonized Brazil in the 16th century; Africans brought to Brazil as slaves; various other European and Middle Eastern, as well as Japanese and other Asian immigrant groups who have settled in Brazil since the mid-19th century; and indigenous peoples of Tupi and Guarani language stock. Intermarriage between the Portuguese and indigenous people or slaves was common. Although the major European ethnic stock of Brazil was originally Portuguese, subsequent waves of immigration have contributed to a diverse ethnic and cultural heritage.

4 According to the passage, which of the following immigrant groups first arrived in Brazil in the 16th century?

- (A) Japanese
- (B) Portuguese
- (C) Middle Easterners
- (D) Indigenous people

Draw Conclusions

Drawing conclusions from information is an important reading skill. You may spend time reading a passage, but what information can you draw from it, and how might you use that information? When an author presents a number of related facts, often you can group those facts in your mind and form a conclusion. A conclusion is a new idea that tells what those facts mean when they are joined together. You have to decide if the facts in a passage support your conclusion the way evidence supports a verdict in a court of law.

Let's take a look at the following passage to see what conclusions can be drawn.

Read the following passage and answer the question.

Preliminary data from NASA's Lunar Crater Observation and Sensing Satellite, or LCROSS, indicate the mission successfully uncovered water in a permanently shadowed lunar crater. The discovery opens a new chapter in our understanding of the moon.

The LCROSS spacecraft and a companion rocket stage made twin impacts in the crater that created a plume of material from the bottom of a crater that has not seen sunlight in billions of years. The plume traveled at a high angle beyond the rim and into sunlight.

"We're unlocking the mysteries of our nearest neighbor," said Michael Wargo, chief lunar scientist at NASA Headquarters in Washington. "The moon harbors many secrets, and this has added a new layer to our understanding."

Scientists long have speculated about the source of significant quantities of hydrogen that have been observed at the lunar poles. The LCROSS findings are shedding new light on the question with the discovery of water, which could be more widespread and in greater quantity than previously suspected. If the water that was formed or deposited is billions of years old, these polar areas could hold a key to the history and evolution of the solar system, much as an ice core sample taken on Earth reveals ancient data. In addition, water and other compounds represent potential resources that could support future lunar exploration.

Which of the following statements can be concluded from the passage?

Ⓐ Water on the moon is only found in places without sunlight.

Ⓑ Having water on the moon can be useful to future moon landings.

Ⓒ Ice cores can show the moon's volcanic origins.

Ⓓ In the future astronauts won't need to bring a water supply when they explore the moon.

There is no evidence that water on the moon is found only in permanently dark places, so choice A is not correct. There is no mention in the passage of ice cores taken from the moon, so choice C is not right. Since we are just beginning to learn about water on the moon, there is no evidence that there is enough to support future astronauts, so choice D is not right. However, the passage does indicate that the presence of water in some amount might be helpful to future moon landings. The correct answer is choice B.

Related Skills: 1, 2, 3, 4

Draw Conclusions

Test Yourself

1 *Read the passage and answer the question. Circle the letter of your choice.*

A new scientific study shows concentrations of toxic chemicals in fish tissue from lakes and reservoirs in nearly all 50 U.S. states. For the first time, the government is able to estimate the percentage of lakes and reservoirs nationwide that have fish containing potentially harmful levels of chemicals such as mercury and PCBs.

These results reinforce the call for revitalized protection of our nation's waterways and long-overdue action to protect the American people. "We are aggressively tackling the issues the report highlights," says a government official. "Before the results were even finalized, the government initiated efforts to further reduce toxic mercury pollution and strengthen enforcement of the Clean Water Act—all part of a renewed effort to protect the nation's health and environment."

The data showed mercury concentrations in game fish exceeding recommended levels in 49 percent of lakes and reservoirs nationwide, and PCBs in game fish at levels of potential concern in 17 percent of lakes and reservoirs. These findings are based on a comprehensive national study.

Which of the following conclusions is justified from the information in the passage?

Ⓐ Fish cause health problems in humans.

Ⓑ Our pollution of the environment is creating toxins in fish.

Ⓒ Fish are creating toxins that are harmful to our lakes and reservoirs.

Ⓓ One shouldn't eat fish caught in nearly all lakes in the US.

2 *Read the passage and answer the question. Circle the letter of your choice.*

Our life in the backwoods was simple and natural; we had few luxuries, but we also had few cares. In our kitchen gardens, potatoes, cabbages, onions, tomatoes, Indian corn, and numerous other vegetables grew most luxuriantly; and of fruits we had great abundance. We lived a natural life and were content. The loom and the spinning-wheel, though they had by this time largely disappeared from the towns, still had a place in every farmhouse. We raised our own food and made our own clothing, often woven by the women on their homemade looms. We breakfasted by the light of a tin lamp fed with lard, four o'clock being a not unusual hour, dined at noon, supped at five, and went to bed with the chickens.

Which of the following conclusions is justified from the information in the passage?

Ⓐ The author believed that life was good in the backwoods.

Ⓑ The food that could be grown by the family was very limited.

Ⓒ The author did not like living in towns.

Ⓓ The family sold their fruits and vegetables to earn a living.

Identify the Feeling or Mood of the Passage

A movie can make you feel happy or sad or angry. The movie director and actors work purposely to make you feel that way. In the same way, the author of a reading passage may use words to make you feel a certain way or to put you into a certain mood. A reading passage can convey an emotion or a mood, just like a movie.

Authors use various words in their writings to evoke feelings in the reader. Surely in your various readings, you have felt happy, shed tears, been frightened, felt nervous, experienced sadness, felt triumphant, or had other feelings. You had those emotions because the author wrote in a certain way, using certain words, to make you feel "caught up in the moment."

When you read a book or an article or even a short reading passage, check in with your feelings. The emotions you feel (presuming they are the ones that the author intended) are what is called the mood of the passage.

Here is an example.

Read the following paragraph and see how you feel while reading it.

> There, under the shade of the sycamores, on my father's old farm, I used to dream of the years to come. I looked through a vista blooming with pleasures, fruited with achievements, and beautiful as the cloud-isles of the sunset. The siren, ambition, sat beside me and fired my young heart with her prophetic song. She dazzled me, and charmed me, and soothed me, into sweet fantastic reveries. She touched me and bade me look into the wondrous future. The bow of promise spanned it. Hope was enthroned there and smiled like an angel of light. Under that shining arch lay the goal of my fondest aspirations.

❶ The mood of this passage is best described as:

   Ⓐ suspicious

   Ⓑ tense

   Ⓒ warm

   Ⓓ frightened

In this passage the author is trying to get you to share the feeling of enjoying a happy memory by using words like *pleasures, wondrous, dazzled, sweet, angel,* and the like to convey a comfortable, warm feeling. You are not frightened by the words, nor do they make you feel tense or suspicious, so choices A, B, and D are wrong. The passage gives you a nice warm feeling. Choice C is correct.

Identify the Feeling or Mood of the Passage

Test Yourself!

1 *Read the passage and answer the question. Circle the letter of your choice.*

The moment that Dixon entered the short winding tunnel that led to the outer air he was vaguely aware that something was wrong. There was a strange and intangibly sinister quality in the moonlight that streamed dimly into the winding passage. Even the cool night air itself seemed charged with a subtle aura of brooding evil.

Dixon reached the end of the tunnel and stepped out into the full radiance of the moonlight. He stopped abruptly and stared around him in utter amazement.

High in the eastern sky there rode the disc of a full moon, but it was a moon weirdly different from any that Dixon had ever seen before. This moon was a deep and baleful green. It was glowing with a stark malignant fire like that which lurks in the blazing heart of a giant emerald! Bathed in the glow of the intense green rays, the desolate mountain landscape shone with a new and eerie beauty.

The mood of this passage is best described as:

Ⓐ Cheerful
Ⓑ Joyful
Ⓒ Sad
Ⓓ Menacing

Circle the words in the paragraph above that help set the mood.

2 *Read the paragraph and answer the question. Circle the letter of your choice.*

In person, Uncle Juvinell is stout and well-rounded. His legs are fat, and rather short; his body is fat and rather long; his belly is snug and plump; his hands are plump and white; his hair is white and soft; his eyes are soft and blue; his coat is blue and sleek; and over his sleek and dimpled face, from his dimpled chin to the very crown of his head—which, being bald, shines like sweet oil in warm firelight—there beams one unbroken smile of fun, good humor, and love, that fills one's heart with sunshine to behold. Indeed, to look at him and be with him a while, you could hardly help half believing that he must be a twin-brother of Santa Claus, so closely does he resemble that far-famed personage, not only in appearance, but in character also; and more than once, having been met in his little sleigh by some belated school-boy, whistling homeward through the twilight of a Christmas or New Year's Eve, he has been mistaken for the jolly old saint himself.

The mood of this passage is best described as:

Ⓐ Cheerful
Ⓑ Sad
Ⓒ Indifferent
Ⓓ Fearful

Circle the words in the paragraph above that help set the mood.

Focus on the Order of Events

One common purpose for reading is to learn how to do something. For example, you can learn how to cook a certain dish by reading a recipe, or how to operate a computer by reading a user's manual. Or you may read in order to understand the steps in a process, such as how an automobile engine works or how to apply for a loan from a bank. In this kind of reading, it is important to understand the sequence of the events that are described. When you are following a recipe, you need to know what to do first, second, or third. When you are trying to learn how an engine functions, you need to understand what happens first, what happens next, and what happens last.

Often on the ASVAB you may be asked to do this kind of reading. For example, you may read a set of directions and then be asked what to do after a certain step in the process. For this kind of reading, pay close attention to the order of the steps or events that are described. Make sure you are reading critically and focusing on details.

Here is an example.

Read the passage and answer the item.

Getting Your First Passport

STEP 1: Complete and Submit Form DS-11: *Application For A U.S. Passport*

Complete Form DS-11: Application for a U.S. Passport. To submit Form DS-11, you:

- **Must** apply **in person** at an Acceptance Facility or Passport Agency
- **Must** include the additional **documentation** required by Form DS-11 (See Steps 2-5)
- **Must not** sign the application until instructed to do so by the Acceptance Agent
- **Must** provide your SSN in accordance with 26 U.S.C. 6039E

STEP 2: Submit Evidence of U.S. Citizenship

When applying for a U.S. passport in person, evidence of U.S. citizenship must be submitted **with** Form DS-11. All documentation submitted as citizenship evidence will be **returned** to you. These documents will be delivered with your newly issued U.S. passport or in a separate mailing.

STEP 3: Present Identification

When applying for a U.S. passport in person, acceptable **identification** must be presented **at the time of application.**

Which of the following is true?

Ⓐ You must sign the application before seeing an agent.
Ⓑ You will receive your passport after submitting the application.
Ⓒ When you get your passport, you will submit your Social Security number.
Ⓓ You must give your identification to the agent to get an application form.

The passage indicates that you must follow the steps in this process in the following order: (1) fill out the application, (2) do not sign it until instructed to do so, (3) present proof of citizenship, (4) provide your social security number, and (5) receive your passport at a later time. The only correct answer is choice B.

Focus on the Order of Events

Test Yourself!

❶ *Read the passage and answer the question. Circle the letter of your choice.*

I woke up this morning to a bright sky and a breathtaking mountain view out my bedroom window. I looked for the newspaper, then went to the kitchen and started the coffee maker. I felt very hungry so I made myself some scrambled eggs with some toast and potatoes. When I finished breakfast I took my vitamins and washed them down with a glass of freshly squeezed orange juice. Leaving the dishes in the sink, I showered, got dressed, and went off to work.

Which of the following lists the correct sequence?

Ⓐ Looking at the mountain view, making breakfast, drinking orange juice, showering

Ⓑ Looking for the newspaper, squeezing orange juice, going off to work, looking at the mountain view

Ⓒ Eating breakfast, showering, noticing the mountain view, going off to work

Ⓓ Taking vitamins, making scrambled eggs, leaving the dishes in the sink, going off to work

❷ *On the lines provided, copy the following sentences in the proper order for the events described.*

I underlined the important points. After a few hours, I tested my knowledge of dates and people in the Civil War. I was worried about scoring well on my history test. I found a comfortable place to study and settled in for a long session. Opening my history book to Chapter 12, I started reading.

_____

_____

_____

_____

_____

Writers have various reasons for writing. Sometimes the purpose is simply to record events. At other times the purpose is to inform readers about something, perhaps an interesting person, place, or idea. One writer might write in order to spur readers to take some action. Another writer might write in order to make readers feel afraid of something. A writer might write in order to entertain, to give an opinion on a topic, to instruct, or to present a different point of view.

When you read something, think about the reason the writer has decided to craft that particular text.

Let's look at an example.

Read the passage and answer the item.

The Internet gives buyers access to a world of goods and services, and gives sellers access to a world of customers. Unfortunately, the Internet also gives con artists the very same access. But being on guard online can help you maximize the global benefits of electronic commerce and minimize your chance of being defrauded. When you go online

- Know who you're dealing with. In any electronic transaction, independently confirm the other party's name, street address, and telephone number.
- Resist the urge to enter foreign lotteries. These solicitations are phony and illegal.
- Delete requests that claim to be from foreign nationals asking you to help transfer their money through your bank account. They're fraudulent.
- Ignore unsolicited emails that request your money, credit card or account numbers, or other personal information.
- If you are selling something over the Internet, don't accept a potential buyer's offer to send you a check for more than the purchase price, no matter how tempting the plea or convincing the story. End the transaction immediately if someone insists that you wire back funds.

What is the author's purpose in writing this passage?

Ⓐ Entertain
Ⓑ Warn
Ⓒ Scold
Ⓓ Describe

Clearly the author is trying to warn readers of certain dangers that exist on the Internet along with all of the potential opportunities. The purpose of this passage to alert readers to potential ways they can get in trouble when they "surf" the Internet or use it to buy and sell products. The passage does describe those dangers, but the best answer is choice B.

Related Skills: 3, 4, 5

Identify the Author's Purpose

Test Yourself!

1 *Read the passage and answer the question. Circle the letter of your choice.*

Wildlife experts and government officials from India and the United States met at India's famed Ranthambore tiger reserve in early November to discuss ways to counter the factors driving one of the world's most iconic animals toward extinction.

Poaching and shrinking habitat are the chief causes of tiger losses. Figures published by the Wildlife Institute of India indicate that the Indian tiger population is dwindling rapidly. There are possibly as few as 1,300, down from an estimated 3,600 five years ago. It's only a matter of time before all the tigers disappear from the planet and it will be our fault if we don't act.

Poverty and affluence are intersecting root causes. The demand for tiger parts comes chiefly from manufacturers of traditional Chinese medicines, for which wild tiger parts are prized ingredients. Tiger skins are increasingly popular in Tibet, where they are worn as status symbols. Growing Chinese affluence has resulted in greater demand.

Impoverished poachers in tiger ranges rely on killing tigers for a living. Human population growth in range states and resulting habitat encroachment is another contributing factor.

As members of the Wildlife Protection Society, we need your dedication and support to save this important animal species. Please write your government representatives to ask that the U.S. become involved in saving the tiger. This is a problem that needs immediate attention before it's too late.

Which of the following best reflects the main purpose of the author in this passage?

Ⓐ Entertain
Ⓑ Cause action
Ⓒ Inform
Ⓓ Create fear

2 *Read the passage and answer the question. Circle the letter of your choice.*

Perhaps it was only because Mark's nerves were on edge that he grew aware at that point in his reflections of two minor signals from his senses. One was that the smell of ammonia, which he had almost stopped noticing, was becoming stronger. The other was the faintest of sounds—a whispering suggestion of motion somewhere behind him. But here in the storage vault nothing should have moved, and Mark's muscles were tensing as his head came around. Almost in the same instant, he flung himself wildly to one side, stumbling and regaining his balance as something big and dark slapped heavily down on the floor at the point where he had stood.

Which of the following best reflects the main purpose of the author in this passage?

Ⓐ Entertain
Ⓑ Cause action
Ⓒ Inform
Ⓓ Create fear

Circle the words in the passage above that you think help to convey the author's purpose.

Distinguish between Facts and Opinions

A very important skill for critical reading is the ability to distinguish between fact and opinion, and between fact and fiction. You've read about Elvis sightings and about persons who say they have spoken with visitors from other galaxies. You've read people's opinions on which weight loss technique you should follow. Stories and articles like these may be written as if they were absolutely true and scientifically proven. But that doesn't mean that they are facts.

You need to be smart about what you are reading. You need to distinguish between opinions (no matter how convincingly stated) and facts. For example, "bananas cost 79 cents per pound at the local supermarket" is a fact. But "bananas taste good" is an opinion because not everyone might agree with that idea. Another example is "Avatar was the best movie ever." You may believe this to be true, but other people might think another movie was much better. It's all a matter of opinion.

Here are some statements.

Determine if each one are is a fact or an opinion by checking the box.

Statement	Fact	Opinion
1. Pumpkin pie tastes better than apple pie.		
2. A day on earth is equal to one rotation of the planet.		
3. Mountain climbing is the most dangerous of all sports.		
4. Blonds have more fun.		
5. The American flag has 50 stars.		
6. The military is the most respected occupation.		
7. All elected officials are corrupt.		
8. This compact car gets better gas mileage than that SUV.		
9. My new computer cost $445.		
10. Our football team is the best in the country.		
11. Steak is more delicious than chicken.		
12. Getting adequate calcium helps your bones stay stronger.		

Answers:

Statement 1: Opinion

Statement 2: Fact

Statement 3: Opinion

Statement 4: Opinion

Statement 5: Fact

Statement 6: Fact (based on polls)

Statement 7: Opinion

Statement 8: Fact

Statement 9: Fact

Statement 10: Opinion

Statement 11: Opinion

Statement 12: Fact

Related Skills: 4, 5, 8

Distinguish between Facts and Opinions

Test Yourself!

❶ Identify the sentences that are fact and those that are opinion in the following paragraph. Write the numbers of the sentences on the lines below

① Family history research is a fascinating pastime. ② In some cultures, family members can trace their lineage back more than a thousand years! ③ Research has shown that throughout the last decade, widespread use of technology and the Internet have fueled significant advancements in the field of genealogy making it more popular now than ever before. ④ I think the best place to start to track your family history is to view the records of Ellis Island.

Sentences that are facts: _____

Sentences that are opinions: _____

❷ Identify the sentences that are fact and those that are opinion in the following paragraph. Write the numbers of the sentences on the lines below.

① The World War II Navajo Code Talkers are perhaps the best-recognized American Indian military figures. ② About 400 Navajo Indians served with the U.S. Marines, mostly in the Pacific theater, transmitting secret tactical messages over military telephone or radio communications networks using codes built on their native language. ③ The National Museum of the American Indian points out that the Code Talkers had to memorize 17 pages of code as part of their training. ④ It was the only battlefield code never broken by the enemy. ⑤ Historians who have studied the event state unequivocally that were it not for the Navajos, the Marines would never have taken Iwo Jima.

Sentences that are facts: _____

Sentences that are opinions: _____

❸ Identify the sentences that are fact and those that are opinion in the following paragraph. Write the numbers of the sentences on the lines below.

① Texting while driving, like talking on cell phones while driving, should be banned by federal law. ② There is heightened concern about the risks of texting while driving, because texting combines three types of distraction—visual, taking the eyes off the road; manual, taking the hands off the wheel; and cognitive, taking the mind off the road. ③ Nearly 6,000 people died in 2008 in crashes involving a distracted or inattentive driver, and more than half a million were injured. ④ Research also shows that the most frequent offenders are the youngest and least-experienced drivers, men and women under 20 years of age.

Sentences that are facts: _____

Sentences that are opinions: _____

Paraphrase to Understand What You Are Reading

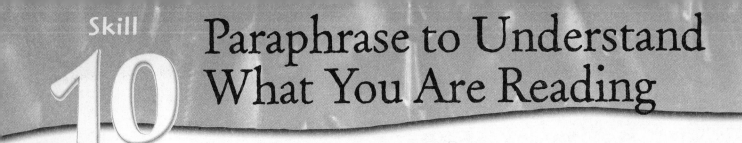

Paraphrasing means putting someone else's idea, writing, or statement into your own words. It's a new way of saying the same thing. When you paraphrase a statement, you express the meaning of that statement in different words that usually make the original meaning clearer to you.

Your ability to paraphrase what you hear or read is a good indicator of whether you understood what was said or what you read.

The act of paraphrasing can help you monitor how well you comprehend what you read or hear. It may even help you better remember what you read because you are using your own words, not the original author's.

As you read paragraphs on the ASVAB, think about how you would paraphrase the information.

Here is an example.

Original Paragraph: Foodborne illness is a serious public health threat. Each year, approximately 76 million cases of foodborne illness occur in the United States alone, according to the Centers for Disease Control and Prevention (CDC). Of those cases of foodborne illness, more than 325,000 people are hospitalized and about 5,000 deaths occur.

Possible Paraphrase: Millions of people are struck with foodborne illness and many die or are hospitalized as a result. This is a serious situation and a threat to public health. Millions of cases of foodborne illness are identified each year.

Here's another example.

Original Paragraph: Studies of homes lost and saved in the wild fires of 1985 and 1998 have led to advances in our understanding of how to protect homes and communities from fire. A big lesson learned from these recent wildfires is that local firefighting agencies will not be able to protect every home during a large wildfire because so many more homes are being built "in the woods." It is now clear that everyone—from homeowners and local leaders to state and federal agencies—must share the responsibility of preventing and preparing for wildfires.

Possible Paraphrase: Both homeowners and fire officials have the responsibility to protect their homes and communities from fires. This is a lesson that has been learned from recent wildfire studies. Many more homes are now being built in wooded areas, and in a wildfire, local firefighting agencies can't protect all of them.

Related Skills: 2, 4, 5, 7, 9

Paraphrase to Understand What You Are Reading

Test Yourself!

1 *Read the passage and rewrite it in your words.*

Original Passage: Architects are searching for natural methods to heat and cool homes. For adaptation to changing temperatures they are looking to the flexible pinecone. Shut tight in the cold, pinecones open their scales to release their seeds when temperatures warm up. Researchers are looking for materials that change shape depending on the level of moisture in the air, opening to shunt warm moist air outside and closing to prevent warm moist air from getting inside.

Possible Paraphrasing: (write your answer here)

_____

_____

_____

_____

2 *Read the passage and write it in your words.*

Original Passage: As the public's faith in the soundness of financial institutions continued to plummet, the nation's banks began to collapse. Although the East Coast was hardest hit—with bank closures in New York, Philadelphia, Baltimore, and elsewhere—bank failures also reached across the Missouri River to cities such as Omaha. The climax came on October 14—Suspension Day—when banking was suspended in New York and throughout New England.

Possible Paraphrasing: (write your answer here)

_____

_____

_____

_____

Compare and Contrast

Critical reading includes the ability to compare and contrast. These two skills involve determining how things that you read about are alike and how they are different. When you *compare*, you identify a particular way in which two or more things are alike, or similar. When you *contrast*, you identify a particular way in which two or more things are different. Sometimes it helps to make a chart to find similarities and differences.

Here is an example.

When you say the word *football*, it has a different meaning depending on where in the world you are. In the United States, football is a game played most often in college and in professional leagues. Players use an elliptical ball called a football. In American football, each team has 11 players on the field at any one time. The way to score points is for a player to physically carry the ball over the goal line. A player who does this makes a "touchdown," which is worth six points. The team with the most points wins. The sport is a contact sport with players colliding with one another to prevent the forward movement of the ball by the opposing team.

In other parts of the world, the term *football* describes what Americans call soccer. It is played by two teams of 11 players each. The object of the game is to drive a circular ball into the opposing team's goal to score one point. The team with the most points wins. To prevent the opposing team from scoring points, a goal keeper on each team tries to block the ball from entering his/her team's goal. Goal keepers can use their hands to catch the ball, but they are the only players who can use their hands. Other players must use their feet to kick the ball or sometimes use their head or torso to intercept and move the ball. Physical contact between players is minimal.

Topic	American Football	Soccer
Number of Players on Team	11	11
Type of Ball	Elliptical	Circular
Number of Points per Score	6	1
Ways Players Handle the Ball and	Physical with hands and carrying	Moving ball with head torso or by kicking
How to Determine Winner	Team with most points	Team with most points
Physical Contact between Players	Physical contact common	Physical contact minimal

So based on the passage, the two sports are alike in the number of players on the team and how to determine the winning team. They are different in the type of ball used, the number of points per score, how the ball is moved or handled, and the amount of physical contact between and among players.

Related Skills: 9, 10

Compare and Contrast

Test Yourself!

1 *Identify the similarities and differences in the following passage by writing "Yes" or "No" for each item in the chart.*

When President Barack Obama was elected, he promised his daughters that they would have a puppy in the White House. Because one of his daughters has allergies, they needed to find a hypoallergenic variety. The choice came down to two types of dogs, a Labradoodle or a Portuguese Water Dog.

As a breed, the Portuguese Water Dog dates back to at least the thirteenth century. Dogs of this kind worked on boats to help Portuguese fisherman. Their feet are somewhat web-like, giving them more traction on the boat decks. The Portuguese Water Dog doesn't shed much, but it needs a lot of exercise because it is a high-spirited dog with lots of energy. It is a very friendly dog and is good with families. It thrives on having a lot of attention.

The Labradoodle is a relatively new breed that was introduced around 1989. It is a cross between a poodle and a Labrador, thus the name Labradoodle. It is a bubbly creature and is good with families. It does not require as much exercise and attention as a Portuguese Water Dog, and it is very sociable with other animals and very patient with young children. Dogs of this kind are very easy to train.

Topic	Labradoodle	Portuguese Water Dog
Hypoallergenic?		
Good with Families?		
Needs a Lot of Attention?		
Needs a Lot of Exercise?		
New Breed of Dog?		

Did you ever hear the phrase "read between the lines"? That is what making inferences is all about. When you make an inference, you read the author's words, but then you combine that information with your own knowledge from experience or reading to figure out what the author is really saying. Your inference is what you think the author really means but did not say straight out.

An inference may be something quite simple. For example, you may see an advertisement for a computer at a special sale price. Nothing in the ad says so directly, but you may easily infer that the sale price is lower than the regular retail price. Making an inference may also require some logical thought. For example, an ASVAB reading passage might say that people who do not engage in some form of physical activity are at greater risk of developing health problems. From this you might infer that people who exercise are likely to enjoy better health.

Let's take a more complex example.

Read the following passage and answer the question.

When the explosive volcano Mt Pinatubo in the Philippines sent tons of ash into the atmosphere, temperatures cooled around the world by about 1.5 degrees for almost two years. Scientists studied three explosive eruptions of different sizes in Indonesia—Tambora, Krakatau, and Agung. They observed decreases in atmospheric temperatures after the eruptions by about the same amount for each eruption—around one degree. The amount of material injected into the stratosphere, however, differed greatly. This made them believe that volcanic ash did not totally drive atmospheric cooling.

Perhaps the most severe volcano-related climate change was associated with a largely nonexplosive eruption that produced very little ash—the 1783 eruption of Laki in Iceland. The eruption lasted 8–9 months and extruded basaltic lava over a large area of the country but very little ash. A bluish haze of sulfur aerosols all over Iceland destroyed most summer crops in the country; the crop failure led to the loss of 75% of all livestock and the deaths of 24% of the population The bluish haze drifted east across Europe during the winter of 1783–1784, which was unusually severe.

In the future, satellites measuring various particles in the atmosphere will be able to associate measurements of atmospheric particles with various changes in climate.

Which of the following can be inferred from the passage?

Ⓐ Atmospheric cooling seems to be associated with sulfur aerosols.
Ⓑ Explosive volcanoes cool the atmosphere by around one degree.
Ⓒ Volcanic ash is needed in order to create noticeable climate change.
Ⓓ Climate warming and cooling are unpredictable

Based on the paragraph, it is clear that some volcanoes are explosive, sending particles high up into the atmosphere, with some effect on the climate. Others are not so explosive but have dramatic effects on the climate. The difference seems to be in the sulfur aerosols. Choice A is the correct answer.

Related Skills: 4, 5, 7, 8, 9

Make Inferences

Test Yourself!

1 *Read the following passage and answer the question. Circle the letter of your choice.*

Although the Scarecrow had been on Silver Island only a few days, he had already instituted many reforms, and thanks to his cleverness the people were more prosperous than ever before. Cheers greeted him wherever he went, and even old Chew Chew was more agreeable and no longer made bitter remarks to Happy Toko. The Scarecrow himself, however, had four new wrinkles and was exceedingly melancholy. He missed the carefree life in Oz, and every minute that he was not ruling the island he was thinking about his old home and dear, jolly comrades in the Emerald City.

Which of the following statements can be inferred from the passage?

Ⓐ The Scarecrow would be happier back with his friends in Oz.
Ⓑ Chew Chew was a grumpy cat.
Ⓒ Living on the island made people get wrinkles.
Ⓓ In Emerald City the people were not prosperous.

2 *Read the following passage and answer the question. Circle the letter of your choice.*

Bells jangled discordantly. A whistle split the air with a piercing note. A band blared away on the platform. With a growing rumble of sound, the Presidential special slowly gathered headway. The President waved a final farewell to the crowds at the platform and sat down. He chatted cheerily with his companions until the train was clear of Charleston, then rose, and with a word to the others stepped into the car.

The United States Secret Service officer slumped back in his chair with a sigh of relief.

"Thank Goodness, that's over," he said. "I was never so glad to get him safely away from a place in my life."

The second Secret Service officer nodded in agreement. The military aide to the President looked up inquiringly.

Which of the following statements can be inferred from the passage?

Ⓐ The President was vacationing in Charleston but had to return home by train.
Ⓑ The President was in some danger in Charleston.
Ⓒ The Secret Service officers did not like traveling by train.
Ⓓ The President did not have enough protection from his military aides.

Use Context Clues to Understand Unfamiliar Words

On the ASVAB your ability to read and understand text is critically important. Many questions are based on reading passages. In order to understand the reading passage, you must know the meaning of the vocabulary that is being used. If you don't know the words, you will be a poor reader and score low on the verbal section of the ASVAB. There are literally many thousands of words in the English language. No one can be expected to know them all, but you will need to know many words to score high on the vocabulary section of the ASVAB. There is no way of predicting which words you will be asked to know. The very best way to build your vocabulary is to read, read, and read some more. Eventually that will increase the number of words you know, and you will do better on any test.

When reading, you will likely encounter words you don't know. Many times the surrounding sentence or sentences will give you good hints that you can use to correctly guess the word's meaning. These hints are called *context clues*.

Here is an example. Read this sentence.

Sanjay was <u>reluctant</u> to leave his house in the raging blizzard as it was dangerous to drive.

Perhaps you don't know the meaning of *reluctant*, so you look at the remainder of the sentence to determine what that word could possibly mean. The first thing you notice is that the weather and driving conditions were bad. Second, apparently Sanjay was thinking about leaving his house, but the bad weather was negatively affecting his plans. So right off, you know that *reluctant* does not mean "happy" to leave the house or "pleased" to leave the house. *Reluctant* must mean that Sanjay was hesitating or rethinking his plans because of the bad weather. So you can conclude that *reluctant* probably means something like "not enthusiastic" to leave the house. The sentence gave you a clue to the meaning of the word. This is called a context clue.

An ASVAB test question might look something like this.

Which of the following words means the same as the underlined word in this sentence?

In order to calm the passengers, Clyde tried to exchange the <u>haggard</u> look on his face for one of competent self-assurance.

Ⓐ Tired
Ⓑ Happy
Ⓒ Clown-like
Ⓓ Sparkling

It appears that the passengers were nervous or upset about something and Clyde wanted to calm them. He wanted to look self-assured, but his face was giving the opposite impression at the moment. So under those circumstances it is doubtful that the way he looked was either "sparkling," "clown-like," or "happy." *Haggard* must mean "tired." If you selected choice A, you would be correct.

Use Context Clues to Understand Unfamiliar Words

Test Yourself!

1 Which of the following words means the same as the underlined word in this sentence? Circle the letter of your choice.

The black clouds let loose a <u>deluge</u> of water that flowed through the open window.

- Ⓐ Drop
- Ⓑ Flood
- Ⓒ Mist
- Ⓓ Sprinkle

2 Which of the following words means the same as the underlined word in this sentence? Circle the letter of your choice.

A silence <u>ensued</u> after the argument, but conversation struck up again when Caroline saw the birds in the cage.

- Ⓐ Stopped
- Ⓑ Started
- Ⓒ Hurt
- Ⓓ Rang out

3 Which of the following words means the same as the underlined word in this sentence? Circle the letter of your choice.

There was a <u>perceptible</u> and refreshing coolness in the air now after the suffocating and oppressive heat.

- Ⓐ Lasting
- Ⓑ Dreary
- Ⓒ Noticeable
- Ⓓ Unwanted

4 Which of the following words means the same as the underlined word in this sentence? Circle the letter of your choice.

Sandi was an <u>ardent</u> lover of animals and abhorred cruelty to them.

- Ⓐ Indifferent
- Ⓑ Absent
- Ⓒ Common
- Ⓓ Passionate

5 Which of the following words means the same as the underlined word in this sentence? Circle the letter of your choice.

Unlike his quiet and low-key cousins, Brian is <u>garrulous</u>.

- Ⓐ Funny
- Ⓑ Inquisitive
- Ⓒ Chatty
- Ⓓ Nasty

6 Which of the following words means the same as the underlined word in this sentence? Circle the letter of your choice.

After the long movie, the friends <u>appeased</u> their hunger at one of the fast food establishments in the neighborhood.

- Ⓐ Satisfied
- Ⓑ Increased
- Ⓒ Craved
- Ⓓ Continued

Know Root Words

A lot of words in the English language are made up of a base word with either a prefix (Skill 15) or a suffix (Skill 16) added to it. The base word has a meaning, and its meaning is changed in some way by adding a prefix or a suffix.

The words *prefix* and *suffix* are really good examples of this. In the word *prefix*, *fix* is the base word, and it means "to fasten or attach." The letter group *pre-* (which is a prefix) means "before." So when *pre-* is attached to the base word *fix*, the resulting word *prefix* means "a word part that is attached before [a root word]." The letter group *suf-* means "below or behind," so when *suf-* is attached to the root word *fix*, the resulting word *suffix* means "a word part that is attached behind [a root word]."

By learning root words, you will able to understand the meaning of many other words in which root words are combined with prefixes or suffixes.

Here are some examples.

Root Word	Meaning	Words That Include the Root Word
audi/audio	Hear	Audience—people who listen to a concert or lecture Audible—can be heard Audiovisual—directed at a person's senses of hearing and sight
astro/aster	Star or Outer Space	Astronaut—person traveling to the stars Asterisk—star-like symbol Asteroid—object floating in space Astronomer—person who studies stars and outer space
bene	Good or Well	Beneficial—having a good effect Benefactor—person who gives money for a cause Benevolent—showing kindness
derm	Skin	Dermatologist—skin doctor Pachyderm—animal with a thick skin Dermatitis—infection of the skin
causor/caust	Burn	Caustic—can burn or burn away Cauterize—burn with a hot instrument
mal	Bad	Malaria—bad air Malicious—acting with ill or bad intent
flora	Flower	Florist—person who works with flowers Flora—plant life in a specific geographic area

Related Skills: 13, 15, 16

Know Root Words

Test Yourself!

For the following items, see if you can list at least one word that includes the root word given. Write your words on the lines provided.

	Root Word	Meaning	Example Word
1	cari/cardio	heart	
2	chron/chrono	time	
3	cline	lean	
4	cogn/cogni	know	
5	cycl	circle or ring	
6	dent	teeth	
7	geo	globe, land, Earth	
8	inter	between	
9	lumin	light	
10	omni	all	
11	pod	foot	

There are hundreds of root words that are commonly used in the English language; only a few are presented in this chapter. Reading as much as you can will help you build your vocabulary. As you read, try to identify the root word and see if you can think of other words that are similar.

Recognize Prefixes and Their Meanings

Prefixes are letter groups that are placed at the beginning of a word to change or alter its meaning in some way. A prefix modifies a word to create another word or thought.

For example, the prefix *pre-* means "before." If you add the prefix *pre-* to the word *view*, you get a new word, *preview*, which means "to see before." If you *preview* a movie, perhaps you are seeing it before it officially opens. For another example, suppose you add the prefix *pre-* to the word *condition*. The new word *precondition* means "a condition or requirement that was set beforehand." For example, a background check might be a precondition for getting hired as a security guard. Not all words that start with *pre-* convey the idea of "before" or "ahead," but many do. So using *pre-* as a prefix with certain root words creates many other words in our language.

But *pre-* isn't the only prefix. Here are a few others that are very helpful to know.

Prefix	Meaning	Example Words
anti–	opposing, against, the opposite	anti–aircraft
circum–	around	circumference
counter–	opposition, opposite direction	counteract
dis–	remove, negate	disbar
dys–	ill, difficult, bad	dysfunctional
extra–	outside, beyond	extraterrestrial
In–/im–	into	incorporate
inter–	between	intergalactic
micro–	small	microclimate
macro–	large	macroeconomics
mono–	one, single	monologue
over–	excessively, completely	overconfident
over–	on top of, above	overcoat

Related Skills: 13, 14

Recognize Prefixes and Their Meanings

Prefix	Meaning	Example Words
poly-	many, several	polygon
post-	after	postgraduate
pro-	favoring, in support of/before	pro-American
proto-	first	prototype
pseudo-	false	pseudoscience
re-	again	repeat
retro-	back	retroactive
sub-	under	substandard
trans-	across	trans-Atlantic
ultra-	beyond, extreme	ultra-marathon

Examples

Here are some sentences from the reading passages in the previous sections of this book in which prefixes were used to alter the meaning of a word. Each of the words with prefixes is bolded so that you can see it.

- If you want to get rid of your old computer, options include **recycling**, **reselling**, and donating.
- Many scientific studies have identified a relationship between elevated levels of fine particles and **increased** illness and **premature** death from heart and lung **disorders**, such as asthma and bronchitis.
- The song's rousing **refrain recalls** the early struggles of a nation.
- The only object more **reflective** is Enceladus, a geologically active moon of Saturn whose surface is continuously **recoated** with highly **reflective** ice by active geysers.
- These results **reinforce** the call for **revitalized** protection of our nation's waterways and long-**overdue** action to protect the American people.
- The **Internet** gives buyers access to a world of goods and services, and gives sellers access to a world of customers.
- It's only a matter of time before all the tigers **disappear** from the planet and it will be our fault if we don't act.
- It is now clear that everyone—from homeowners and local leaders to state and federal agencies—must share the responsibility of **preventing** and **preparing** for wildfires.

Recognize Prefixes and Their Meanings

Test Yourself!

For each prefix listed in the table, think of some additional words that include that prefix. Write the words in the column on the right.

Prefix	Meaning	Words That Include the Prefix
anti–	opposing, against, the opposite	
circum–	around	
counter–	opposition, opposite direction	
dis–	remove, negate	
dys–	ill, difficult, bad	
extra–	outside, beyond	
in–/im–	into	
inter–	between	
micro–	small	
macro–	large	
mono–	one, single	

Recognize Prefixes and Their Meanings

Prefix	Meaning	Words That Include the Prefix
over–	excessively, completely	
over–	on top of, above	
poly–	many, several	
post–	after	
pro–	favoring, in support of/before	
proto–	first	
pseudo–	false	
re–	again	
retro–	back	
sub–	under	
trans–	across	
ultra–	beyond, extreme	

Recognize Suffixes and Their Meanings

A suffix is a letter or a group of letters added to the end of a word that alters its meaning in some way. There aren't as many suffixes as prefixes, but they are important to know.

Here are some examples of suffixes and how they can change word meanings.

- Adding the suffix *-ful* to the root word *joy* makes the new word *joyful*, or "full of joy."
- Adding the suffix *-able* to the root *read* creates the new word *readable*, meaning "able to be read."
- Adding the suffix *-ly* to the adjective *quick* makes the adverb *quickly*, meaning "in a quick way."

Here is a listing of common suffixes. It may be helpful for you to memorize this list.

Suffix	Meaning	Example Word
-able	able to be	preventable
-acity (-ocity)	quality of	veracity, velocity
-age	action or process	carnage
-ance	state or quality of	brilliance
-ate	makes it a verb	procrastinate
-crat	person with power	bureaucrat
-er	more	bigger
-escence	condition, state or process	adolescence
-est	most	smartest
-ible	able to be	legible
-ish	like something	brutish
-less	without	homeless

Related Skills: 13, 14

Recognize Suffixes and Their Meanings

Suffix	Meaning	Example Word
-like	similar to/resembling	childlike
-ly	in the manner of	significantly
-ology	study of	biology
-or	person who	inventor
-phobia	fear of	acrophobia
-ship	having the skill of	authorship
-ular	relating to or resembling	muscular
-ward	in the direction of	backward

Here are some suffixes used in sentences in the reading passages in previous chapters in this book. They are bolded for you to see.

- The way to score points is for a player to **physically** carry the ball over the goal line.
- It is a very **friendly** dog and is good with families.
- Although the use of high-speed Internet is growing **faster** among **older** people, the **percentage** of high-speed users is **larger** in the **younger** generation.
- The amount of material injected into the stratosphere, however, differed **greatly**.
- A **bluish** haze of sulfur aerosols all over Iceland destroyed most summer crops in the country.
- The Scarecrow himself, however, had four new wrinkles and was **exceedingly melancholy**.
- He chatted **cheerily** with his companions until the train was clear of Charleston.
- So given that, it doesn't seem like the way he looked now was sparkling, **clown-like**, or happy.

Recognize Suffixes and Their Meanings

Test Yourself!

For each of the following suffixes, think of some additional words that include the suffix. Write the words in the column at the right.

Suffix	Meaning	Words That Include the Suffix
-able	able to be	
-acity (-ocity)	quality of	
-age	action or process	
-ance	state or quality of	
-ate	makes it a verb	
-crat	person with power	
-er	more	
-escence	condition, state or process	
-est	most	
-ible	able to be	
-ish	like something	
-less	without	
-like	similar to/resembling	

Recognize Suffixes and Their Meanings

Suffix	Meaning	Words That Include the Suffix
-ly	in the manner of	
-ology	study of	
-or	person who	
-phobia	fear of	
-ship	having the skill of	
-ular	relating to or resembling	
-ward	in the direction of	

Synonyms are critically important if you want to score high on the ASVAB. The Word Knowledge test is made up entirely of questions that require you to know the meaning of various words. Each question asks you to find the synonym for a given word.

What exactly is a synonym? A *synonym* is a word that has the same or nearly the same meaning as another word. So for example, think about the word *create*. What word means the same or almost the same as *create*? Some synonyms for *create* could be *make*, *produce*, *formulate*, *build*, or *construct*. Each of these words is a synonym for the word *create*.

So how do you learn synonyms? You learn them by reading and by using the dictionary to look up the meaning of words that you don't know. You learn synonyms by listening to people talk and hearing them use different words to communicate the same or similar ideas. You learn synonyms by creating word lists and memorizing the meaning of the words. You learn synonyms by using an unfamiliar word correctly in a sentence. You learn synonyms by checking out root words and identifying any prefixes or suffixes that are used.

All the skills covered in the Reading section of this book will help you with the ASVAB, but several skills will help you with the Word Knowledge test in particular. These skills are Use Context Clues (Skill 13), Know Root Words (Skills 14), Recognize Prefixes (Skill 15), and Recognize Suffixes (Skill 16). This skill, Identify Synonyms, will give you more practice in knowing the meaning of words. Because this skill is so important, this section will be much longer than the other skills.

You will find questions on the ASVAB that are like this.

---

1. The word <u>wisdom</u> most nearly means

     Ⓐ Wish
     Ⓑ Understanding
     Ⓒ Lacking
     Ⓓ Scenic

The best synonym for the word *wisdom* is *understanding*. Other possible synonyms could be *insight* or *knowledge*.

2. The word <u>humorous</u> most nearly means

     Ⓐ Funny
     Ⓑ Sad
     Ⓒ Bent
     Ⓓ Truthful

The best synonym for the word *humorous* is *funny*. Other possible synonyms are *amusing* or *comical*.

Identify Synonyms—Part 1

Other questions on the ASVAB will look like this:

---

3. From reading his application form, it was clear that he was <u>eligible</u> for the position.

Ⓐ Accepted
Ⓑ Rejected
Ⓒ Qualified
Ⓓ Perfect

Eligible most nearly means *qualified*. Other synonyms would be *suitable* or *appropriate*.

4. Kurt looked at his little sister in her fanciest dress and was <u>captivated</u> by what he saw.

Ⓐ Shocked
Ⓑ Displeased
Ⓒ Fascinated
Ⓓ Happy

The word *captivated* most nearly means *fascinated*. Other synonyms could be *charmed* or *enthralled*.

Test Yourself!

Find the best synonym for each of the underlined words. Circle the letter of your choice.

❶ The Civil War went a long way toward <u>abolishing</u> the practice of slavery.

Ⓐ Prohibiting
Ⓑ Explaining
Ⓒ Promoting
Ⓓ Supporting

❷ The capability of the least expensive computer was <u>adequate</u>, so she purchased it.

Ⓐ Sufficient
Ⓑ Inexpensive
Ⓒ Unknown
Ⓓ Explained

❸ Sam's <u>ailment</u> was not so severe that he needed to be hospitalized right away.

Ⓐ Temper
Ⓑ Temperature
Ⓒ Condition
Ⓓ Sickness

❹ Jason preferred <u>contemporary</u> furniture over the styles favored by his parents' generation.

Ⓐ Colorful
Ⓑ Modern
Ⓒ Unique
Ⓓ Significant

Identify Synonyms—Part 1

5 After hours in the car, we were <u>famished</u> when we reached the restaurant.

Ⓐ Chilly
Ⓑ Disappointed
Ⓒ Weary
Ⓓ Hungry

6 The <u>desecration</u> of the flag was an act that could not be forgiven.

Ⓐ Ruin
Ⓑ Folding
Ⓒ Hoisting
Ⓓ Washing

7 James was happy to <u>achieve</u> his purpose after so many days of trying.

Ⓐ Admire
Ⓑ Reduce
Ⓒ Control
Ⓓ Accomplish

8 During the storm, the shutter <u>detached</u> from the window of the beach cottage.

Ⓐ Separated
Ⓑ Swung
Ⓒ Connected
Ⓓ Hailed

9 He was <u>earnest</u> in his desire to make the world a better and safer place.

Ⓐ Weak
Ⓑ Overt
Ⓒ Sincere
Ⓓ Halting

10 She daydreamed about an exciting <u>escapade</u> on a distant tropical island.

Ⓐ Contribution
Ⓑ Adventure
Ⓒ Sail
Ⓓ Walk

11 The word <u>dismiss</u> most nearly means

Ⓐ Reject
Ⓑ Inspect
Ⓒ Supervise
Ⓓ Warn

12 The word <u>feasible</u> most nearly means

Ⓐ Possible
Ⓑ Foolish
Ⓒ Movable
Ⓓ Happy

Related Skills: 11, 12, 13, 14, 15, 16, 18

Identify Synonyms—Part 1

⑬ The word <u>flourish</u> most nearly means

ⓐ Suffer
ⓑ Contain
ⓒ Deteriorate
ⓓ Thrive

⑭ The word <u>fundamental</u> most nearly means

ⓐ Extreme
ⓑ Cautious
ⓒ Basic
ⓓ Prosperous

⑮ The word <u>placid</u> most nearly means

ⓐ Calm
ⓑ Intense
ⓒ Destructive
ⓓ Meek

⑯ The word <u>immune</u> most nearly means

ⓐ Susceptible
ⓑ Resistant
ⓒ Reclusive
ⓓ Worldly

⑰ The word <u>irresistible</u> most nearly means

ⓐ Frigid
ⓑ Determined
ⓒ Folksy
ⓓ Tempting

⑱ The word <u>monotonous</u> most nearly means

ⓐ Frivolous
ⓑ Boring
ⓒ Amusing
ⓓ Wise

⑲ The word <u>paradoxical</u> most nearly means

ⓐ Logical
ⓑ Withdrawn
ⓒ Inconsistent
ⓓ Mechanical

⑳ The word <u>perforate</u> most nearly means

ⓐ Penetrate
ⓑ Rectify
ⓒ Justify
ⓓ Praise

Because the ASVAB Word Knowledge test is so important in determining whether you are accepted into the military, this lesson gives you more vocabulary-building practice. Word Knowledge questions test your ability to identify synonyms, so the exercise below is designed to help you sharpen this skill.

The following set of words are good candidates for you to study. These are words that most high school students are expected to know. Study the meanings listed for each word, especially for words that are unfamiliar to you.

Word	Meaning	Word	Meaning
astonishing	astounding	strenuous	laborious
systematic	orderly	annoyance	irritation
conscientious	careful	tendency	inclination
fundamental	basic	accumulate	gather
observation	inspection	courteous	considerate
maneuver	scheme	analogous	corresponding
undoubtedly	certainly	temperament	personality
influential	powerful	tranquility	serenity
corresponding	matching	perseverance	persistence
mischievous	playful	obstacle	impediment
interpretation	explanation	permissible	allowed
sacrilegious	irreverent	accessible	available
repetition	repeating	haphazard	random
incredulous	disbelieving	feasible	possible
prevalent	common	intervene	come between
inflammable	able to burn	cynical	skeptical
synthesis	mixture	discriminate	distinguish
privilege	special right	melancholy	sad
opposition	resistance	illogical	irrational
conjunction	combination	sufficient	enough
treacherous	disloyal	symmetrical	balanced
recognition	identification	tyranny	oppression
preference	penchant		

Identify Synonyms—Part 2

Test Yourself!

For each of these words, provide at least one synonym. Write the synonym or synonyms in the column on the right.

Word	Meaning	Synonym(s)
astonishing	astounding	
systematic	orderly	
conscientious	careful	
fundamental	basic	
observation	inspection	
maneuver	scheme	
undoubtedly	certainly	
influential	powerful	
corresponding	matching	
mischievous	playful	
interpretation	explanation	
sacrilegious	irreverent	
repetition	repeating	
incredulous	disbelieving	
prevalent	common	
inflammable	able to burn	

Identify Synonyms—Part 2

Word	Meaning	Synonym(s)
synthesis	mixture	
privilege	special right	
opposition	resistance	
conjunction	combination	
treacherous	disloyal	
recognition	identification	
preference	penchant	
strenuous	laborious	
annoyance	irritation	
tendency	inclination	
accumulate	gather	
courteous	polite	
analogous	corresponding	
temperament	personality	
tranquility	serenity	
perseverance	persistence	
obstacle	impediment	

Identify Synonyms—Part 2

Word	Meaning	Synonym(s)
permissible	allowed	
accessible	available	
haphazard	random	
feasible	possible	
intervene	come between	
cynical	skeptical	
discriminate	distinguish	
melancholy	sad	
illogical	irrational	
sufficient	enough	
symmetrical	balanced	
tyranny	oppression	

Build Your Vocabulary

It is said that to be a competent reader, you need to understand 50,000 to 75,000 words. These are words you learn over time both in and out of school. They are words you pick up as you read a variety of books, magazines, documents, and publications.

There is no predicting what words you will be asked to know on the ASVAB. The best approach is to add many words to your vocabulary. This will not only help you on the test, but it will also make understanding your training manuals and instructors much easier.

The best thing to do is to learn some common words that are typical of high school students, such as the ones below.

Words			
abhor	conduit	impetus	ostracize
abominable	confiscate	incentive	panacea
abrasion	consensus	incinerate	pariah
acrimonious	copious	incongruous	perennial
adjudicate	courteous	insinuate	perilous
affiliate	culpable	interlude	perishable
affinity	deteriorate	jeopardize	pertinent
allegiance	disseminate	latent	pinnacle
altruism	eccentric	legacy	poignant
ambivalent	emancipate	legitimate	precedent
ameliorate	enumerate	loiter	predominant
belligerent	equivocate	lucrative	premonition
benign	eradicate	magnanimous	profusion
blatant	exacerbate	mediate	prominent
boisterous	facsimile	menace	propensity
cadence	flammable	mindless	proximity
catharsis	forfeit	morbid	ratify
cessation	formidable	nebulous	recalcitrant
circuitous	germane	negligent	reconcile
clandestine	gullible	novice	refurbish
coalition	heretic	obtrusive	reminisce
compatible	hesitant	omnipotence	renegade
concentric	imagine	oscillate	rescind

Build Your Vocabulary

Words			
resilient	spontaneous	taunt	tumultuous
retaliate	sporadic	tenacious	ubiquitous
rigorous	squalid	tenuous	unscrupulous
sanguine	stringent	testimonial	velocity
sedentary	subsidiary	trajectory	vicarious
simultaneous	superfluous	translucent	voracious
sleuth	susceptible	trepidation	whimsical
solvent	taut	truncate	zealous

Test Yourself!

For each of these words, write a short definition in the space provided.

Word	Definition
abominable	
abrasion	
acrimonious	
adjudicate	
affiliate	
allegiance	
altruism	
ambivalent	
belligerent	
blatant	
boisterous	
cadence	
cessation	
circuitous	
coalition	
compatible	
concentric	
confiscate	
consensus	
courteous	
culpable	
deteriorate	

Build Your Vocabulary

Word	Definition
disseminate	
eccentric	
emancipate	
enumerate	
eradicate	
exacerbate	
facsimile	
forfeit	
formidable	
germane	
gullible	
hesitant	
impetus	
incentive	
incinerate	
incongruous	
insinuate	
jeopardize	
latent	
legacy	
legitimate	
magnanimous	
mediate	
menace	
morbid	
nebulous	
negligent	
obtrusive	
oscillate	
ostracize	
panacea	
perennial	
perilous	
perishable	
pertinent	
pinnacle	
precedent	

Related Skills: 13, 14, 15, 16, 17, 18

Build Your Vocabulary

Word	Definition
predominant	
premonition	
prominent	
propensity	
proximity	
ratify	
recalcitrant	
reconcile	
refurbish	
reminisce	
rescind	
resilient	
retaliate	
sanguine	
sedentary	
simultaneous	
sleuth	
spontaneous	
sporadic	
squalid	
stringent	
superfluous	
susceptible	
taut	
tenacious	
tenuous	
testimonial	
trajectory	
translucent	
trepidation	
truncate	
tumultuous	
ubiquitous	
vicarious	
voracious	
whimsical	

Know (No) Your Homonyms

Homonyms. Just looking at the prefix of this word, you might suspect that it has to do with things that are the same. If you thought that, you would be exactly correct! Homonyms are words that sound the same but are spelled differently and mean different things. Here is a good example: *to, too, two.* The word *to* means "toward" or "in the direction of," as in the sentence "I am going <u>to</u> the store." The word *too* means "also," as in the sentence "I like cake and chocolate ice cream <u>too</u>." *Too* also means "in excess," as in "That band was playing music <u>too</u> loudly." Finally, *two* is the number, as in the sentence "I bought <u>two</u> books."

Knowing about homonyms is important because it helps build and refine your vocabulary.

The chart below lists a few common homonyms. Once you learn to recognize homonyms, you'll start noticing many more in the words people use every day.

Homonym Sets	Word Meanings
aid	to help
aide	an assistant
air	gas we breathe
heir	person who will inherit
aisle	narrow walkway
I'll	contraction of *I will*
isle	island
allowed	permitted
aloud	spoken to be heard
ascent	climb
assent	agree
ate	past tense of *eat*
eight	the number 8
aural	deals with hearing
oral	deals with the mouth and speaking
bald	without hair
bawled	cried out loud
band	musical group
banned	forbidden
bare	without clothes
bear	animal
berry	fruit
bury	hide underneath something

Related Skills: 13, 14, 15, 16, 17, 18, 19

Know (No) Your Homonyms

Homonym Sets	Word Meanings
base	bottom or foundation
bass	stringed instrument or deep/low tone
bases	as in baseball
basis	starting point; foundation
be	exist
bee	insect

Test Yourself!

Read the sentence and indicate which of the homonyms should be used. Circle the letter of your choice.

1 We had a wonderful time building sandcastles on the _____.

Ⓐ beach
Ⓑ beech

2 We danced to the _____ of the music.

Ⓐ beet
Ⓑ beat

3 We found the lost watch in the trash _____.

Ⓐ been
Ⓑ bin

4 The evening sky was a bright _____.

Ⓐ blue
Ⓑ blew

5 He and his pals went hunting for wild _____.

Ⓐ bore
Ⓑ boar

6 We heard the story so many times that we were _____.

Ⓐ bored
Ⓑ board

7 After he started studying karate, he become much _____ in his dealing with bullies.

Ⓐ boulder
Ⓑ bolder

8 He pumped the _____ to stop the car on the icy road.

Ⓐ brake
Ⓑ break

Know (No) Your Homonyms

⑨ Even though it was a sensitive subject, I decided to _____ the issue with her.

Ⓐ brooch
Ⓑ broach

⑩ At the end of our visit, I waved good- _____.

Ⓐ by
Ⓑ bye
Ⓒ buy

⑪ The tourists visited the US _____ building in Washington DC.

Ⓐ capital
Ⓑ capitol

⑫ With her inheritance, she purchased a two _____ diamond ring.

Ⓐ carrot
Ⓑ carat
Ⓒ karat

⑬ The _____ of gardenias filled the room.

Ⓐ scent
Ⓑ cent
Ⓒ sent

⑭ The musician strummed a _____ on his guitar.

Ⓐ cord
Ⓑ chord
Ⓒ cored

⑮ The architect chose the _____ for the new building on the highest point of the hill.

Ⓐ sight
Ⓑ site
Ⓒ cite

⑯ His explanation didn't seem to have a _____ of truth to it.

Ⓐ kernel
Ⓑ colonel

⑰ Her face turned pink when he gave her that _____.

Ⓐ compliment
Ⓑ complement

⑱ It was amazing to see so many _____ in the park.

Ⓐ dear
Ⓑ deer

⑲ The teacher tried hard to _____ a response from the shy child.

Ⓐ elicit
Ⓑ illicit

⑳ It was the _____ time that the mistake was made.

Ⓐ forth
Ⓑ fourth

Related Skills: 13, 14, 15, 16, 17, 18, 19

㉑ The horse had an unusual _____ as it trotted down the field.

   Ⓐ gait
   Ⓑ gate

㉒ She was _____ down the path by her guide dog.

   Ⓐ lead
   Ⓑ led

㉓ Because the taxes were not paid, the agency put a _____ on his property.

   Ⓐ lien
   Ⓑ lean

㉔ His shirt was so short that his _____ showed.

   Ⓐ navel
   Ⓑ naval

㉕ The athlete was careful not to _____ his exercise after the last injury.

   Ⓐ overdo
   Ⓑ overdue

Know Your Antonyms

In earlier lessons you dealt with synonyms, words that have the same meaning as another word. *Antonyms* are just the opposite. The antonym of a word is a word that has the opposite meaning. Think of the word *love*; what is its opposite? Yes, it's *hate*. Think of the word *finish*. Its antonym is *start*. What about the antonym of *minor*? Yes, it's *major*.

Why do you need to know antonyms? If you can identify the antonym of a word, that shows that you know what the original word means. Knowing antonyms builds your vocabulary and helps you learn new words. It helps you score well on the ASVAB, particularly on the Paragraph Comprehension and Word Knowledge tests, but also on other tests that require knowing words.

Here are some examples of antonyms. When you read the original word, see if you can think of the antonym before reading the answer.

Word	Antonym
absence	presence
always	never
answer	question
abundant	scarce
artificial	natural
attractive	repulsive
begin	end
blunt	sharp
bitter	sweet
build	destroy; demolish
captive	free
conceal	reveal
discourage	encourage
ebb	flow
economize	waste
encourage	discourage

When you look at the list above, notice that if you think of the word in the right-hand column as the original word, the word in the left-hand column becomes its antonym.

Know Your Antonyms

Test Yourself!

For each of the following words listed in the left hand column, write at least one antonym in the column on the right.

Word	Antonym
entrance	
excited	
export	
feeble	
freedom	
frank	
generous	
gloomy	
harmless	
hasten	
horizontal	
inferior	
intentional	
loyal	
maximize	
minority	
optimist	
permanent	
sorrow	
success	
transparent	
vacant	
voluntary	

Watch for Words That Are Often Confused

Some people claim that the English language is difficult to learn because there are many words that are easily confused for each other, and people often mistakenly use one word in a particular situation when a different word is required.

For example, people often use the words *less* and *fewer* incorrectly. The word *less* is used in referring to something that can't be counted. Conversely, *fewer* is used when something can be counted.

"I completed the job <u>in less time</u> than George took to do it" is the correct use of the word *less*. "I completed the job <u>in fewer hours</u> than George took to do it" is also correct. Time is a concept that can't be counted, but hours or minutes certainly can be counted.

Here is another example:

Correct: There is <u>less fog</u> today than yesterday. (You cannot count fog.)
Correct: There were <u>fewer foggy days</u> this month than last. (You can count foggy days.)

Affect and *effect* are another pair of words that are very commonly misused. *Affect* is a verb that means "to act on" or "to produce a change in." *Effect* is a noun that means "a result or consequence."

Incorrect: The vitamin pill I added to the soup did not <u>effect</u> its taste.
Correct: The vitamin pill I added to the soup did not <u>affect</u> its taste.

Incorrect: The drought is having a bad <u>affect</u> on our crops.
Correct: The drought is having a bad <u>effect</u> on our crops.

There are many words like these that can trip people up as they are reading, speaking, or writing. See how good you are at choosing the correct word.

Test Yourself!

Read each sentence and select the word that should be used to make the sentence correct. Circle the letter of your choice.

❶ They all came to the theater **accept/except** the lead actor.

    Ⓐ Accept

    Ⓑ Except

❷ The salesperson made an **allusion/illusion** to the computer problems that were typical of that brand.

    Ⓐ Allusion

    Ⓑ Illusion

❸ The decorations were **all ready/already** taken down before his surprise arrival.

    Ⓐ All ready

    Ⓑ Already

Watch for Words That Are Often Confused

4 Her husband, an **eminent/imminent** psychiatrist, received a lifetime achievement award.

Ⓐ Eminent
Ⓑ Imminent

5 The dog started barking as soon as **its/it's** master left the house.

Ⓐ Its
Ⓑ It's

6 Because of the weight loss, his pants were **lose/loose**.

Ⓐ Lose
Ⓑ Loose

7 It's time to **precede/proceed** to the next step in the sequence.

Ⓐ Precede
Ⓑ Proceed

8 It's time to **right/write** the autobiography of my life.

Ⓐ Right
Ⓑ Write

9 His **conscience/conscious** told him not to follow through with his plans.

Ⓐ Conscience
Ⓑ Conscious

10 His score on the ASVAB was higher **then/than** that of any of his classmates.

Ⓐ Then
Ⓑ Than

11 He was about to **accept/except** the package when he saw it was not meant for him.

Ⓐ Accept
Ⓑ Except

12 When he was in trouble, he went to his father for some **advice/advise**.

Ⓐ Advice
Ⓑ Advise

13 Kurt is going to **borrow/lend** me his leather jacket for the weekend party.

Ⓐ Borrow
Ⓑ Lend

14 **Where/were** is the nearest fast food restaurant?

Ⓐ Where
Ⓑ Were

15 The magician was **thru/threw/through/thorough** with his act at the birthday celebration.

Ⓐ Thru
Ⓑ Threw
Ⓒ Through
Ⓓ Thorough

Add and Subtract Accurately

If you have trouble adding and subtracting, you will find the math sections of the ASVAB/AFQT to be very troublesome. Not only must you be accurate, but you must also be quick. You should know the answers to simple addition and subtraction questions without even thinking.

Test Yourself!

Get a stopwatch or a wristwatch with a second hand, and see how long it takes you to answer the following addition and subtraction items.

Add the following.

1
  5
+ 7

2
  7
+ 8

3
  9
+ 3

4
  9
+ 8

5
  12
+ 17

6
  13
+ 18

7
  28
+ 67

8
  49
+ 57

9
  104
+ 509

10
  999
+ 888

11
  476
+ 983

12
  1,257
+ 984

13
  9
+ 7

14
  87
+ 42

15
  649
+ 899

16
  12
+ 13

17
  15
+ 17

18
  642
+ 712

19
  84
+ 94

20
  509
+ 603

21
  893
+ 234

22
  481
  381
+ 289

23
  779
  212
+ 487

24
  764
  389
  312
+ 1,344

Add and Subtract Accurately

㉕
```
  1,473
  2,890
  4,129
+ 8,114
```

㉖
```
  2,114
  3,478
  1,129
+ 5,584
```

㉗
```
  1,310
  1,487
  3,012
  5,674
+ 8,911
```

㉘
```
     14
    112
  2,178
+ 4,391
```

Subtract the following.

㉙
```
  12
-  7
```

㉚
```
  33
- 27
```

㉛
```
  99
- 27
```

㉜
```
  504
- 304
```

㉝
```
  901
- 497
```

㉞
```
  912
- 212
```

㉟
```
  1,298
-   989
```

㊱
```
  294
- 283
```

㊲
```
  2,767
-   948
```

㊳
```
  3,499
- 2,888
```

㊴
```
  7,679
- 5,889
```

㊵
```
  98,774
- 89,999
```

How long did it take you to do these? If it took more than 5 minutes, you are moving too slowly.

Check your answers to these problems on page 171. If you got more than one wrong, you need to be more careful.

Try the questions again, and this time, try to shave off at least 10 seconds from your time.

Multiply Whole Numbers

As with addition and subtraction, when multiplying whole numbers you must be accurate and quick with your calculations. You need to be totally comfortable with the multiplication tables. If you are slow with any of this or make mistakes, your score on the math tests will be low.

Here is the multiplication table. You absolutely must have this down cold. Memorize it to give yourself the confidence needed to score well on the math items.

Multiply…

By This

This ⟨

x	0	1	2	3	4	5	6	7	8	9	10	11	12
0	0	0	0	0	0	0	0	0	0	0	0	0	0
1	0	1	2	3	4	5	6	7	8	9	10	11	12
2	0	2	4	6	8	10	12	14	16	18	20	22	24
3	0	3	6	9	12	15	18	21	24	27	30	33	36
4	0	4	8	12	16	20	24	28	32	36	40	44	48
5	0	5	10	15	20	25	30	35	40	45	50	55	60
6	0	6	12	18	24	30	36	42	48	54	60	66	72
7	0	7	14	21	28	35	42	49	56	63	70	77	84
8	0	8	16	24	32	40	40	56	64	72	80	88	96
9	0	9	18	27	36	45	54	63	72	81	90	99	108
10	0	10	20	30	40	50	60	70	80	90	100	110	120
11	0	11	22	33	44	55	66	77	88	99	110	121	132
12	0	12	24	36	48	60	72	84	96	108	120	132	144

Test Yourself!

Multiply the following.

❶ 12 × 3 = _____

❷ 7 × 8 = _____

Related Skill: 23

Multiply Whole Numbers

3   8 × 8 = _____

4   9 × 8 = _____

5   23 × 3 = _____

6   66 × 4 = _____

7   123 × 5 = _____

8   123 × 12 = _____

9   98 × 47 = _____

10   1,457 × 99 = _____

11   11 × 12 = _____

12   99 × 78 = _____

13   2,467 × 83 = _____

14   259 × 956 = _____

15   1,459 × 8,773 = _____

Divide Whole Numbers

Another basic arithmetic skill you must know is division. Later on in this book you will work on dividing with fractions, but this skill is about dividing using whole numbers.

Your best bet in improving this skill is to work a lot of practice items. Again, speed is important. The practice items in this section are easier than most you will find on the ASVAB, so if you don't do well on these, start practicing all kinds of division items so that your focus on accuracy and speed is second nature.

Test Yourself!

1 112 ÷ 2 = _____

2 75 ÷ 3 = _____

3 540 ÷ 12 = _____

4 4,575 ÷ 915 = _____

5 51,750 ÷ 1,125 = _____

6 888 ÷ 4 = _____

7 444 ÷ 12 = _____

8 $3\overline{)2{,}691}$ = _____

9 120,296 ÷ 5,468 = _____

10 $97\overline{)45{,}396}$ = _____

11 $198\overline{)90{,}288}$ = _____

12 68 ÷ 5 = _____

13 100 ÷ 3 = _____

Related Skill: 23, 24

Divide Whole Numbers

⑭ 489 ÷ 12 = _____

⑮ 49)1,323 = _____

⑯ 447 ÷ 4 = _____

⑰ 1,224 ÷ 6 = _____

⑱ 1,394 ÷ 12 = _____

⑲ 4,448 ÷ 24 = _____

⑳ 5,478 ÷ 2 = _____

㉑ 86,125 ÷ 125 = _____

㉒ 33,818 ÷ 37 = _____

㉓ 2,793 ÷ 57 = _____

㉔ 12)288 = _____

㉕ 163)5,053 = _____

㉖ 14)3,458 = _____

㉗ 256 ÷ 16 = _____

㉘ 361 ÷ 19 = _____

㉙ 20,757 ÷ 1,221 = _____

㉚ 5,646 ÷ 6 = _____

For the ASVAB, you'll need to know how to add, subtract, multiply, and divide with positive and negative numbers. Positive numbers are numbers that are greater than 0, such as 6 or 142. Negative numbers are numbers that are less than 0, such as –4 or –18. (See the number line below.) The *absolute value* of a number is the distance of the number from 0 on a number line. For example, the absolute value of –12 is 12.

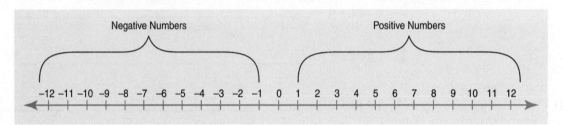

- **To add numbers with the same sign,** add their absolute values. The sum will have the same sign as the numbers you added.

  Examples:

4	27	–97	–16
+9	+32	+(–24)	+(–89)
13	59	–121	–105

- **To add numbers with different signs,** first find their absolute values. Subtract the lesser absolute value from the greater absolute value. Give the sum the same sign as the number with the greater absolute value.

  Examples:

+27	–95	–479	+987
+(–12)	+14	+358	+(–662)
+15	–81	–121	+325

- **To subtract a negative number,** remember that subtracting a negative number is the same as adding a positive number.

  Examples:

+65	+106	–36	–261
–(–32)	–(–58)	–(–24)	–(–97)
+97	+164	–12	–164

- **To multiply and divide negative numbers,** use this simple trick. First treat all the numbers as positive and perform the operation as you normally would. If there is an odd number of negative signs, the answer will be negative. If there is an even number of negative signs, the answer will be positive.

  Examples:

–45	–37	$1{,}260 \div (–12) = –105$	$–368 \div 8 = –46$
× (+3)	× (–2)		
–135	+74		

Related Skills: 23, 24, 25

Work with Positive and Negative Numbers

Test Yourself!

Add:

1 -42
      $+27$

2 -99
      $+12$

3 $-9,999$
         $+1$

Subtract:

4 $+197$
      $-(-100)$

5 -36
      $-(-12)$

Multiply:

6 $29 \times (-12) =$ _____

7 $(-2) \times (-9) =$ _____

8 $(-97) \times (-15) =$ _____

9 $(-3) \times (-3) \times (-3) =$ _____

10 $74 \times (-2) =$ _____

Divide:

11 $66 \div (-3) =$ _____

12 $(-66) \div (-3) =$ _____

13 $100 \div (-4) =$ _____

14 $1,000 \div (-2) =$ _____

15 $-1,000 \div 2 =$ _____

Know Place Values and How to Round

Place Values. Consider the number 32,768,445.123. Each digit in that number has a specific meaning and value. We say that each digit occupies a particular "place." The meaning of the digit is due to the "place" that it occupies. The chart below shows the name of each "place" in the number.

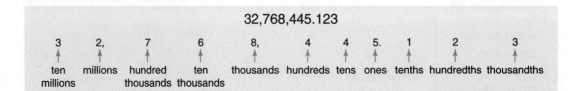

32,768,445.123

3	2,	7	6	8,	4	4	5.	1	2	3
↑	↑	↑	↑	↑	↑	↑	↑	↑	↑	↑
ten millions	millions	hundred thousands	ten thousands	thousands	hundreds	tens	ones	tenths	hundredths	thousandths

- The digit 3 is in the "ten millions" place. It represents three "ten millions"—a very big number.
- The digit 5 occupies the "ones" place. It represents five ones.
- The digits to the right of the decimal point represent quantities that are less than 1. The 3 all the way at the right is in the "thousandths" place. It represents three thousandths—a very small number.

Rounding. Often you will be asked to round to the nearest 10, 100, or 1,000, or to the nearest tenth, hundredth, or thousandth. A good way to do this is to underline the digit in the place to which you are rounding. Identify the digit immediately to the right. If it is 5 or greater, round the underlined digit up by 1. If it is 4 or less, leave the underlined digit as is. Change all the digits to the right of that digit to zeros.

Examples:
- Round 679,123 to the nearest thousand. Underline the digit in the thousands place. That digit is 9. So 679,123 is where you start. Look at the digit in the place immediately to the right. That digit is less than 5, so leave the underlined digit as is. The original number rounded to the nearest thousand is 679,000.
- Round 1,456,488,552.023 to the nearest 100,000. Underline the digit in the hundred thousands place: 1,456,488,552.023. The digit to the right is 8, so you round the underlined digit up by 1. The original number rounded to the nearest 100,000 is 1,456,500,000.
- Round 447.345 to the nearest hundredth. Underline the digit in the hundredths place: 447.346. The digit to the right is equal to or greater than 5, so you round the underlined digit up by 1. The original number rounded to the nearest hundredth is 447.35.

Know Place Values and How to Round

Test Yourself!

1 Round 356,891 to the nearest 10. _____

2 Round 100,000.456 to the nearest tenth. _____

3 Round 845,023 to the nearest thousand. _____

4 Round 234,592,093 to the nearest to thousand. _____

5 Round 234,592,093 to the nearest 10 thousand. _____

6 Round 234,592,093 to the nearest million. _____

7 Round 557,456.0923 to the nearest tenth. _____

8 Round 557,456.0923 to the nearest hundred. _____

9 Round 455.882 to the nearest tenth. _____

10 Round 455.882 to the nearest hundredth. _____

Order Your Operations

In a math calculation that involves more than one operation, you can get different answers depending on the order in which you perform the operations. For example, consider this math problem:

$$\left[4 \times (3+2) - \left(12 \div \frac{4}{2}\right)\right]^2 =$$

Depending on the order in which you multiply, add, subtract, divide, and apply the exponent, you can get different answers. But don't worry. There are specific rules for cases like this, and if you follow them, you will get the correct answer.

Here's what you do. Follow this order:

1. Perform the operations within the parentheses and brackets.
2. Apply the powers or exponents.
3. Multiply and divide in order from left to right.
4. Add and subtract in order from left to right.

So, for the example just shown:

$$[4 \times 5 - (12 \div 2)]^2 =$$

Step 1. Perform the operations within parentheses. Add 3 + 2 in the first parentheses to get 5. Then, in the second parentheses, divide 12 by 2 to get 6. So now the expression becomes:

$$[4 \times 5 - (6)]^2 = (4 \times 5 - 6)^2$$

Step 2. Multiply and divide from left to right, so the expression becomes:

$$(20 - 6)^2$$

Step 3. Add and subtract from left to right, so the expression becomes:

$$14^2 = 196$$

You couldn't apply the exponent before because you hadn't taken care of what was in the parentheses and brackets.

Order Your Operations

Test Yourself!

Solve the following expressions:

1 $(16 - 6)^2 = $ _____

2 $(18 - 5) + (19 + 8) \div 2^2 = $ _____

3 $6^2 - 5^2 + 1 = $ _____

4 $(6 \div 3) \times (8/2) + 22 = $ _____

5 $19 - 8 + 2^2 - 13 = $ _____

6 $(24 - 12)^2 + 18 = $ _____

7 $(6 + 8)^2 + 3^2 = $ _____

8 $(22 - 20)^3 + (9/3) - 10 = $ _____

9 $(4 - 8)^2 - (12 - 15)^2 + 3 = $ _____

10 $(4/2)^2 + (-2)^2 - 13 = $ _____

11 $(10/2)^3 - (12/6)^2 - 15 + 14 = $ _____

12 $[(-10/5)^2 + (-4)^2 - 10]^2 = $ _____

Use Fractions and Decimals

Fractions. Up to now, we have dealt only with whole numbers. Now we will move on to fractions and decimals, which are parts of a whole. Let's tackle fractions first. A fraction is like one piece of your favorite pie, not the whole pie. If you took 1 of 8 equal slices, your slice would be $\frac{1}{8}$ of the pie. The remaining slices would be $\frac{7}{8}$ of the pie. If you took 1 of 4 equal slices, your part would be $\frac{1}{4}$ of the pie. In a fraction, the number on the top is called the *numerator*. The number on the bottom is called the *denominator*.

Reducing Fractions to Lowest Terms. Let's work with $\frac{1}{4}$ for a moment. There are many other fractions that have the same value: $\frac{2}{8}, \frac{3}{12}, \frac{4}{16}, \frac{5}{20}$ and so on. In fact, every fraction in which the bottom number is 4 times larger than the top number is equal to $\frac{1}{4}$. The numbers 1 and 4 are the smallest numbers that represent this 1-to-4 relationship, so for all of these fractions, $\frac{1}{4}$ is said to be in "lowest terms." A fraction is in lowest terms when the numerator and denominator have no common factors other than 1. In ASVAB math problems involving fractions, you are usually asked to express your answer in lowest terms. So it is important to be able to "reduce" fractions by finding the greatest common factor (GCF) of the numerator and denominator and then dividing both terms by their GCF. For example, if the answer to a problem is $\frac{5}{20}$, you need to see that the GCF of 5 and 20 is 5. Dividing both terms by 5 results in the fraction $\frac{1}{4}$.

Decimals. Another way to represent parts of a whole is through decimals. In the decimal system, 0.50 is 5 tenths or 50 hundredths. The decimal 0.25 is 25 hundredths, 0.78 is 78 hundredths, and 0.250 is 250 thousandths. (Go back to Skill 27 for a review of place value if you need it.)

Because fractions and decimals both represent parts of a whole, they are just two ways to represent the same thing. You should know how to convert each one to the other.

- **To convert a fraction to a decimal,** divide the numerator by the denominator. Here is a simple example. Take the fraction $\frac{1}{4}$. Divide the numerator, 1, by the denominator, 4, to get 0.25. For the fraction $\frac{1}{8}$, divide 1 by 8 to get 0.125.

- **To convert a decimal to a fraction,** express the number in terms of tenths, hundredths, thousandths, or a similar fraction based on the number of places in the decimal. Then write the fraction in lowest terms. For example, 0.25 can be converted to $\frac{25}{100}$; reduced to its lowest terms, it is $\frac{1}{4}$. Or take 0.125, which can be converted to $\frac{125}{1000}$; reduced to its lowest terms, it is $\frac{1}{8}$.

Related Skills: 23, 24, 25, 27

Use Fractions and Decimals

Test Yourself!

List these fractions in their lowest terms.

1 $\dfrac{24}{96}$ = _____

2 $\dfrac{19}{57}$ = _____

3 $\dfrac{4}{64}$ = _____

4 $\dfrac{25}{500}$ = _____

Change these fractions into decimals.

5 $\dfrac{24}{96}$ = _____

6 $\dfrac{19}{57}$ = _____

7 $\dfrac{4}{64}$ = _____

8 $\dfrac{25}{500}$ = _____

Change these decimals into fractions.

9 0.75 = _____

10 0.225 = _____

Mixed numbers are combinations of whole numbers and fractions. For example, $1\frac{1}{4}$ is a mixed number. It represents 1 whole + $\frac{1}{4}$, like a whole pie + $\frac{1}{4}$ more.

Converting a Mixed Number to a Fraction. The number 1 can also be expressed as $\frac{4}{4}$, so the number $1\frac{1}{4}$ is the same as $\frac{4}{4} + \frac{1}{4} = \frac{5}{4}$. Let's try another mixed number: $3\frac{1}{2}$.

If 1 is the same as $\frac{2}{2}$, then 3 must be $3 \times \frac{2}{2} = \frac{6}{2}$. Now add: $3\frac{1}{2} = \frac{6}{2} + \frac{1}{2} = \frac{7}{2}$. Let's try one final example. The mixed number $9\frac{2}{3}$ is the same as $\frac{29}{3}$. That's because $9 = 9 \times \frac{3}{3} = \frac{27}{3}$. Now add: $\frac{27}{3} + \frac{2}{3} = \frac{29}{3}$.

There is an easier way to do this calculation. Let's work again with $3\frac{1}{2}$. Multiply the whole number 3 by the fraction denominator 2, then add the fraction numerator 1. Express the result as a fraction with the same denominator as the fraction in the original mixed number. So for $3\frac{1}{2}$, you calculate:

$$3 \times 2 = 6 \text{ and } 6 + 1 = 7, \text{ so } 3\frac{1}{2} = \frac{7}{2}$$

Take $9\frac{2}{3}$ as another example:

$$9 \times 3 = 27 \text{ and } 27 + 2 = 29, \text{ so } 9\frac{2}{3} = \frac{29}{3}$$

Converting a Fraction to a Mixed Number. You can work the same calculation backwards. If you are asked to express $\frac{8}{3}$ as a mixed number, simply divide the numerator 8 by the denominator 3 to get $2\frac{2}{3}$. Similarly, $\frac{22}{4}$ can be expressed as $5\frac{2}{4}$ or $5\frac{1}{2}$. (Don't forget to convert your answers to their lowest terms.)

Converting a Mixed Number to a Decimal. You can also convert mixed numbers to decimals. Take the mixed number, make it into a fraction, then divide the numerator by the denominator to get the decimal. Here are two examples:

$$4\frac{1}{4} = \frac{17}{4} = 4.25$$

$$18\frac{2}{5} = \frac{92}{5} = 18.4$$

Understand Mixed Numbers

Test Yourself!

Change the following mixed numbers into fractions.

1 $5\dfrac{1}{8}$ = _____

2 $10\dfrac{1}{2}$ = _____

3 $16\dfrac{2}{3}$ = _____

4 $9\dfrac{7}{8}$ = _____

Change the following fractions into mixed numbers.

5 $\dfrac{41}{8}$ = _____

6 $\dfrac{21}{2}$ = _____

7 $\dfrac{50}{3}$ = _____

8 $\dfrac{79}{8}$ = _____

Change the following mixed numbers into decimals.

9 $21\dfrac{3}{4}$ = _____

10 $90\dfrac{5}{6}$ = _____

Add and Subtract Fractions, Mixed Numbers, and Decimals

Now that you understand mixed numbers and decimals, let's start using them in mathematical operations.

Add and Subtract Fractions with Different Denominators. Add $\frac{1}{2}$ and $\frac{3}{4}$. Adding fractions with different denominators is like mixing apples and oranges. Before you can add them, you need to rewrite one or both fractions so that they both have the same denominator. You can change $\frac{1}{2}$ to $\frac{2}{4}$; now both fractions have a denominator of 4.

Add the numerators: $\frac{2}{4} + \frac{3}{4} = \frac{5}{4}$. Convert that to a mixed number to get $1\frac{1}{4}$.

Subtract those same numbers: $\frac{2}{4} - \frac{3}{4} = -\frac{1}{4}$. Don't forget the minus sign!

Now let's get a little more complicated. Add $\frac{1}{2}$ and $\frac{2}{3}$. You need to put these fractions into common terms. Convert both to fractions with a denominator of 6. To convert $\frac{1}{2}$ to a fraction with a denominator of 6, you need to multiply the denominator 2 by 3. But if you multiply the denominator of a fraction by a number, you have to multiply the numerator by the same number; otherwise you change the value of the fraction. Multiply both numerator and denominator of $\frac{1}{2}$ by 3 to get $\frac{3}{6}$. Convert $\frac{2}{3}$ to a fraction with a denominator of 6. Multiply both numerator and denominator by 2. The result is $\frac{4}{6}$. Add: $\frac{3}{6} + \frac{4}{6} = \frac{7}{6}$. Change $\frac{7}{6}$ to a mixed number to get $1\frac{1}{6}$.

Add and Subtract Mixed Numbers. Add $3\frac{3}{4}$ and $7\frac{3}{8}$. Add both whole numbers: $3 + 7 = 10$. Then deal with the fractions. As always, you need to put them into common terms. Convert $\frac{3}{4}$ into a fraction with a denominator of 8 by multiplying both numerator and denominator by 2. The result is $\frac{6}{8}$. Now add: $\frac{6}{8} + \frac{3}{8} = \frac{9}{8}$ or $1\frac{1}{8}$. Add that number to the whole number that you calculated previously: $1\frac{1}{8} + 10 = 11\frac{1}{8}$. Let's try subtraction. $7\frac{3}{8} - 3\frac{3}{4}$ is the same as $7\frac{3}{8} - 3\frac{6}{8}$. Subtract the 3 from 7 to get 4. Then subtract the $\frac{6}{8}$ from the $\frac{3}{8}$ to get $-\frac{3}{8}$. Because that fraction is a negative number, you need to subtract it from your whole number total of 4. The number 4 is the same as $3\frac{8}{8}$. Subtract: $3\frac{8}{8} - \frac{3}{8} = 3\frac{5}{8}$.

A second way to perform this calculation is to transform each mixed number into a fraction. $7\frac{3}{8} = \frac{59}{8}$. $3\frac{3}{4} = \frac{15}{4}$ or $\frac{30}{8}$. Then subtract: $\frac{59}{8} - \frac{30}{8} = \frac{29}{8}$ or $3\frac{5}{8}$.

Decimals are easy! Just add or subtract as you would normally. For example: 32.45 + 3.75 = 36.2. Or try 32.45 – 3.75. Subtract as normal to get 28.7.

Add and Subtract Fractions, Mixed Numbers, and Decimals

Test Yourself!

1 $\dfrac{2}{3} + \dfrac{5}{6} =$ _____

2 $\dfrac{2}{3} + \dfrac{3}{4} =$ _____

3 $\dfrac{7}{9} - \dfrac{1}{2} =$ _____

4 $27\dfrac{2}{3} + 5\dfrac{5}{6} =$ _____

5 $27\dfrac{2}{3} - 5\dfrac{5}{6} =$ _____

6 $66.66 + 33.2 =$ _____

7 $66.66 - 33.2 =$ _____

8 $1\dfrac{1}{4} + 3\dfrac{3}{8} =$ _____

9 $1\dfrac{1}{4} - 3\dfrac{3}{8} =$ _____

10 $997.43 - 38.96 =$ _____

11 $4,446.98 + 37.3471 =$ _____

12 $37.34 + 0.947423 =$ _____

13 $0.08041 - 0.02009 =$ _____

14 $3.046 - 2.981 =$ _____

Multiply and Divide Fractions, Mixed Numbers, and Decimals

Multiplication. First let's try a simple example. Multiply $\frac{1}{2} \times \frac{2}{3}$. Multiply the two numerators: $1 \times 2 = 2$. Use the 2 as the new numerator. Multiply the two denominators: $2 \times 3 = 6$. Use the 6 as the new denominator. Your result then is $\frac{2}{6}$. Reduce to lowest terms: $\frac{2}{6} = \frac{1}{3}$.

Now for mixed numbers. Multiply $3\frac{1}{3} \times 6\frac{7}{8}$. Start by transforming each mixed number into a fraction. $3\frac{1}{3} \times 6\frac{7}{8} = \frac{10}{3} \times \frac{55}{8}$. Multiply the two numerators to get 550 and the two denominators to get 24. The resulting fraction is thus $\frac{550}{24}$. Convert this into a mixed number by dividing the numerator by the denominator. The result is $22\frac{22}{24}$. Reducing to lowest terms the final answer is $22\frac{11}{12}$. Multiplying with decimals is a snap. Here is a simple example: 1.5×2.7. The result is 4.05. To place the point correctly, count the digits to the right of the decimal points in the two numbers that you are multiplying. There is a total of two digits, 5 and 7, to the right of those decimal points. Now in the answer, count two places from the right. That is where you place the decimal point: 4.05.

Division. To divide one fraction by another, you just invert the second term and multiply. Here is an example:

$$\frac{1}{2} \div \frac{1}{8} = \frac{1}{2} \times \frac{8}{1} = \frac{8}{2} = 4$$

Here is a more difficult example using mixed numbers:

$$2\frac{3}{4} \div 3\frac{1}{2} = \frac{11}{4} \div \frac{7}{2} = \frac{11}{4} \times \frac{2}{7} = \frac{22}{28}, \text{which reduces to } \frac{11}{14}$$

Dividing decimals is easy because it is straight division. Here is an example: $12.5 \div 8.3$. In the number that you are *dividing by* (8.3), move the decimal point to the right until the number is a whole number (83). Now, in the number that you are *dividing* (12.5), move the decimal point the same number of places to the right. That makes the number 125, or 125.0. Then divide. In your answer, place the decimal point exactly above the decimal point in 125.0. The answer is 1.506, when rounded to the nearest thousandth.

Related Skills: 24, 25, 27, 30, 31

Test Yourself!

1 $\dfrac{2}{3} \times \dfrac{7}{8} =$ _____

2 $1\dfrac{4}{5} \times 2\dfrac{6}{7} =$ _____

3 $3.45 \times 10.2 =$ _____

4 $\dfrac{2}{3} \div \dfrac{7}{8} =$ _____

5 $5\dfrac{7}{8} \div 2\dfrac{1}{4} =$ _____

6 $3.45 \div 2.5 =$ _____

7 $\dfrac{1}{2} \times 3\dfrac{3}{4} =$ _____

8 $0.09 \times 184 =$ _____

9 $6\dfrac{1}{3} \div 2\dfrac{1}{2} =$ _____

10 $12.7 \times 8.1 =$ _____

11 $12.7 \div 8.1 =$ _____

12 $184.12 \times 19.7 =$ _____

Convert between Percents, Fractions, and Decimals

On the ASVAB you are likely to get at least one math question that requires some knowledge of this skill. Keep in mind that *percent* means "how many out of 100." For example, if you took a test that had 100 questions and got 75 correct, you scored 75% ("75 out of 100"). Twenty-five percent (25 out of 100) of your answers were incorrect.

Converting a Percent to a Fraction. Imagine once again that you answered 75 out of 100 test questions correctly. How to you convert your 75% score to a fraction? By definition, a 75% score (75 correct out of 100) is the fraction $\frac{75}{100}$. But remember that on the ASVAB, if your answer is a fraction, it must be in lowest terms. You can see that for the fraction $\frac{75}{100}$, both the numerator and denominator are divisible by 5. So divide: $75 \div 5 = 15$ and $100 \div 5 = 20$, so $\frac{75}{100} = \frac{15}{20}$. But this fraction is still not in lowest terms. You can see that both 15 and 20 are again divisible by 5, so divide: $15 \div 5 = 3$ and $20 \div 5 = 4$. So $\frac{15}{20} = \frac{3}{4}$. Now your answer is finally in lowest terms.

Converting a Percent to a Decimal. This is easy. Remember that your 75% test score means that you answered 75 out of 100 questions correctly. By definition, "75 out of 100" is the decimal 0.75. A score of 63% would be the decimal 0.63.

Converting a Fraction to a Decimal. Now let's convert your $\frac{75}{100}$ test score into a decimal. To do this, as you learned in Skill 29, you simply divide the numerator of the fraction by the denominator. Because $\frac{75}{100} = \frac{15}{20} = \frac{3}{4}$, you can use any one of these fractions for your division. You will get the same answer no matter which one you choose. So for $\frac{3}{4}$, $3 \div 4 = 0.75$. That is the equivalent decimal. For the percent of questions you got wrong, the equivalent decimal is 0.25.

Converting a Decimal to a Fraction. Now let's try going in the opposite direction. Convert the decimal 0.75 to a fraction. By definition, 0.75 means "seventy-five hundredths" or 75 out of 100, which makes it the fraction $\frac{75}{100}$.

For these kinds of questions on the ASVAB, you should be able to make certain percent, decimal, and fraction determinations quickly and by memory. A chart of the most common percent, fraction, and decimal equivalents is provided on page 184 of this book.

Related Skills: 23, 24, 25, 29, 30, 31, 32

Convert between Percents, Fractions, and Decimals

Test Yourself!

1 What is the decimal equivalent of 33%?

_____

2 What is the decimal equivalent of 62.5%?

_____

3 What is the fraction equivalent of 33%?

_____

4 What is the fraction equivalent of 62.5%?

_____

5 What is the fraction equivalent of 85%?

_____

6 What is the percent equivalent of $\frac{4}{5}$?

_____

7 What is the percent equivalent of $\frac{7}{8}$?

_____

8 What is the percent equivalent of 1.2?

_____

Use Exponents and Roots

On the ASVAB and other math tests you may have to solve problems involving exponents and roots. It is important that you understand both concepts. Let's start with exponents.

Exponents. An exponent is a little number positioned just to the right of the top of another number. It tells you to multiply that other number by itself as many times as indicated by the exponent. For example, in the expression 2^6, the "6" is an exponent that tells you to multiply the 2 by itself 6 times. So $2^6 = 2 \times 2 \times 2 \times 2 \times 2 \times 2$. Do the multiplication: $2 \times 2 = 4$

$$4 \times 2 = 8$$

$$8 \times 2 = 16$$

$$16 \times 2 = 32$$

$$32 \times 2 = 64$$

So, $2^6 = 64$.

Let's try another example. What number is 3^4? That would be $3 \times 3 \times 3 \times 3$, or $3 \times 3 = 9$, $9 \times 3 = 27$, and $27 \times 3 = 81$. An exponent can also be referred to as a "power." For example, you might see 3^4 referred to "3 to the 4th power." So, a question on the ASVAB might ask, "What is 3 to the 4th power?" The correct answer is still 81.

Roots. A root is the opposite of an exponent. The root of a given number is another number that, when raised to a certain power, will produce the given number. One common kind of root is the square root. The *square root* of a given number is another number that, when raised to the 2nd power, will produce the given number. For example, the square root of 9 is 3 or –3 because $3 \times 3 = 9$ and $-3 \times -3 = 9$. The positive square root of 9 is shown like this: $\sqrt{9}$. The negative square root of 9 is shown like this: $-\sqrt{9}$.

You may also be asked to find the cube root of a number. The *cube root* of a given number is the number that, when raised to the 3rd power, will produce the given number. For example, the cube root of 27 is 3 because $3 \times 3 \times 3 = 27$. It is written like this: $\sqrt[3]{27}$.

It is helpful to know some typical square roots, as these are likely to appear in problems on the ASVAB and other math tests.

Negative Exponents. What do you do when the exponent is a negative number? For example, what is 3^{-2}? When you see an expression like this, follow this example: $3^{-2} = \dfrac{1}{3^2} = \dfrac{1}{(3 \times 3)} = \dfrac{1}{9}$. Here is another example: $3^{-3} = \dfrac{1}{3^3} = \dfrac{1}{(3 \times 3 \times 3)} = \dfrac{1}{27}$. Don't forget to change the exponent from negative to positive when putting the given number in the denominator of the fraction.

Related Skills: 24, 25, 28

Use Exponents and Roots

Test Yourself!

1 What is 4^2? _____

2 What is 4^4? _____

3 What is $\sqrt{144}$? _____

4 What is the square root of 144? _____

5 What is $\sqrt[3]{343}$? _____

6 What is 6^2? _____

7 What is 3^3? _____

8 What is the cube root of 729? _____

9 What is $\sqrt[3]{729}$? _____

10 What is $\sqrt{576}$? _____

11 What is 4^{-2}? _____

12 What is 8^{-1}? _____

Because very large numbers like 1,245,000,000,000 and very small numbers like 0.00000345692 can be difficult to handle, very often a system called scientific notation is used to make them easier to deal with. *Scientific notation* is a way of writing very large or very small numbers in a more concise form.

Very Large Numbers. To convert 1,245,000,000,000 to scientific notation, rewrite the number as the product of two factors. The first factor is a number greater than or equal to 1 but less than 10. The second factor is a power of 10. Start by moving the decimal point in the original number to the left in order to create the first factor. Count the number of places the decimal point was moved: 12 places. So use 12 as the exponent of the second factor.

$$1.245,000,000,000$$

So 1,245,000,000,000 in scientific notation is written 1.245×10^{12}.

You might also be asked to translate a number written in scientific notation into the standard form of the number. So consider 3.466×10^4. 10^4 indicates that the decimal point was moved 4 places to the left. When you move the decimal point back 4 places to the right, you see that the standard form of the number is 34,660.

Very Small Numbers. Let's use 0.000459. To write this number in scientific notation, move the decimal point to the right just after the 4 in order to create the first factor. Count the number of places the decimal point was moved: 4 places.

So, 0.000459 in scientific notation is written as 4.59×10^{-4}.

Multiplying in Scientific Notation. To multiply two numbers that are in scientific notation, simply multiply the whole numbers and add the exponents. For example:

$$(1.2 \times 10^4) \times (2.7 \times 10^3) = ?$$

Multiply the whole numbers: $1.2 \times 2.7 = 3.24$

Add the exponents: $4 + 3 = 7$

The correct answer is thus 3.24×10^7.

Dividing in Scientific Notation. When dividing numbers that are in scientific notation, you probably would guess that you divide the whole numbers and subtract the exponents. Correct! So:

$$(2.4 \times 10^6) \div (1.2 \times 10^4) = 2 \times 10^2$$

Remember that you need to consider adding and subtracting positive and negative numbers in these calculations!

 Related Skills: 23, 26, 27, 31, 34

Use Scientific Notation

Test Yourself!

1. Transform the number 6.77×10^6 into the standard form of the number.

   _____

2. Transform the number 6.77×10^{-6} into the standard form of the number.

   _____

3. Put the number 0.00000877 into scientific notation.

   _____

4. Put the number 0.00000000000877 into scientific notation.

   _____

5. Put the number 1,233,344,000,000,000,000,000 into scientific notation.

   _____

6. Multiply 3.3×10^{12} by 2.0×10^3.

   _____

7. Divide 4.4×10^5 by 2.2×10^3.

   _____

Identify and Understand the Mean, Median, and Mode

When you work with many numbers, sometimes it's best to summarize that information in a way that tells something important about the numerical information. One common way to do that is to find the mean, median, or mode.

Mean. The mean is the average of all the numbers in a given set. You calculate the average by adding all the numbers together and then dividing by the number of numbers. Here is an example. Look at the following numbers and add them up.

12, 23, 34, 15, 30, 39, 45, 49, 50, 32

The sum of those numbers is 329. To calculate the mean or average, divide by the number of numbers. There are 10 numbers in the set. So 329 ÷ 10 = 32.9.

Here is another example.

34, 45, 35, 35, 14, 39, 50, 52, 65, 70, 57, 35, 44, 23, 35

The sum of those numbers is 633. There are 15 numbers in the set, so the mean is 633 ÷ 15 = 42.2.

Mode. The mode is the number that appears most frequently in a given set of numbers. In the number set we just used, you can see that every number appears just once except for the number 35, which appears 4 times. So the mode of that set is 35.

Median. The median is the middle number in a set of numbers. Let's use that same number set again, but this time, order the numbers from lowest to highest. (You can also order them from highest to lowest—it doesn't matter.)

14, 23, 34, 35, 35, 35, 35, ⟨39,⟩ 44, 45, 50, 52, 57, 65, 70

The middle number in this set is 39, and that is the median. This works out nicely because there is an odd number of numbers. If there is an even number, add the two middle numbers and divide by 2.

Mean, median, and mode each have their uses. The mean or average is especially useful if you want to describe a large set of numbers. But if you have a small set of numbers, the mean does not represent that set very well, especially if one number is much larger or smaller than the other numbers in the set.

Here is an example. What is the mean of the following numbers? 43, 50, 54, 55, 1000. The mean of these numbers is 1202 ÷ 5 or 240.4. Although 240.4 is an accurate mean or average, it is not very helpful as a way of representing that number set, which consists mostly of numbers that are less than 56. In this instance, the median, 54, does a better job of representing the number set. You use the mode if you want to show which number appears most frequently in the number set.

Identify and Understand the Mean, Median, and Mode

Test Yourself!

❶ Calculate the mean of the following number set:

13, 17, 23, 43, 50, 56, 46, 76, 92, 84

Mean: _____

❷ What is the mean of this set of numbers, rounded to the nearest tenth?

55, 88, 45, 67, 33, 45, 56, 100, 120, 200, 158

Mean: _____

❸ Find the median of this set of numbers:

90, 86, 84, 82, 76, 75, 70

Median: _____

❹ Find the median of this set of numbers:

90, 86, 84, 82, 76, 75, 70, 66

Median: _____

❺ What is the mode of this number set?

17, 23, 43, 50, 56, 46, 76, 92, 50, 23, 27 50

Mode: _____

❻ What is the mode of this number set?

17, 23, 76, 43, 50, 56, 46, 76, 92, 50, 23, 27, 50, 76, 50, 76

Mode: _____

Graphs and charts are visual representations of numbers and their relationships to each
other. You are likely to be asked to interpret one on the ASVAB test.

Circle Graph. Look at the following graph, which represents the ice cream flavor
preferences reported in a poll of 165 students at a certain high school. This kind of
graph is called a circle graph or pie graph (because it resembles a pie with slices). Based
on the graph, which flavor was the favorite of the largest group of students who were
polled?

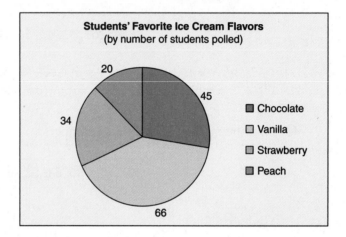

The graph makes it easy to see that the largest group, 66 students, preferred vanilla.

Sometimes the data are presented as percentages of a whole rather than actual
numbers. That is why you always need to pay careful attention to the labels on graphs.
The following circle graph shows the same data, but this time the number labels are
percentages of the total group of 165 students, not the number of individual who
preferred each ice cream flavor.

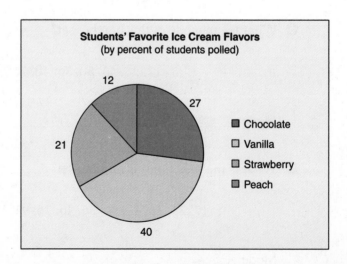

Interpret Charts and Graphs

Bar Graph. Here are the same data shown on a type of graph called a bar graph:

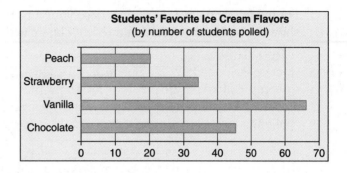

Line Graph. A line graph is typically used to show how data change over time. For example, the following graph shows how the daily high temperature in a certain town changed from day to day during the first 2 weeks of October.

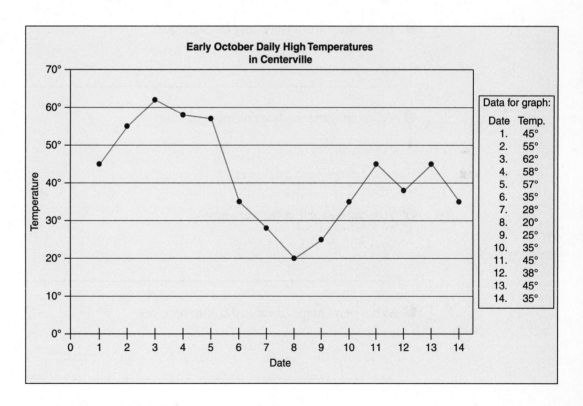

Interpret Charts and Graphs

Test Yourself!

For the following five questions, base your answers on the bar graph below, which shows how students voted in a recent class election.

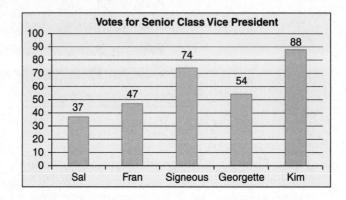

1 How many votes were cast for Signeous?

_____

2 Who obtained the least number of votes?

_____

3 How many total votes were cast?

_____

4 What percentage of votes did Kim receive?

_____

5 How many votes did Georgette and Sal receive together?

_____

Interpret Charts and Graphs

Questions 6 and 7 are based on the following line graph, which shows Lethea's scores on weekly quizzes last semester.

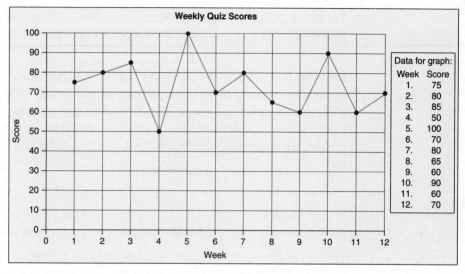

6 In which 2 weeks did Lethea achieve her best scores?

_____

7 What was the Lethea's lowest quiz score during the semester?

_____

Question 8 is based on the following pie graph.

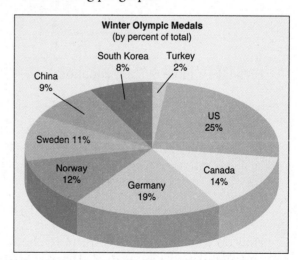

8 Which four countries earned a total of 50% of the Olympic medals?

Ⓐ Canada, Germany, Norway, and Sweden
Ⓑ United States, Canada, China, and Turkey
Ⓒ Germany, Norway, China, and South Korea
Ⓓ Turkey, South Korea, Sweden, and Germany

There will probably be some algebra questions on your ASVAB test, so it's a good idea to spend some time studying basic algebra concepts and practicing solving algebra problems.

Solving Equations. An equation is a math expression in which one quantity or set of quantities is stated to be equal to another. Often one of the quantities in an equation will have an unknown value. This unknown is represented by a letter such as x. Because the quantities in an equation are equal to each other, you can use that equality to *solve* the equation and find the value of the unknown.

Here is a very simple equation:

$$2 + x = 10$$

The unknown number x must have a value that, when added to 2, equals 10. So x must be 8. Normally on the ASVAB and other tests, you won't find such a simple equation.

The usual way to solve this kind of problem is to restructure the equation a bit. To do so, you can add quantities to each side or subtract quantities from each side. Or you can multiply each side by a number or divide each side by a number. But remember: *Whatever you do to one side of an equation, you must do the same to the other side.* Otherwise, the two sides of the equation will no longer be equal!

Your aim when manipulating an equation in this way is to end up with the unknown quantity by itself on one side of the equals sign, and the known numerical quantities on the other side. For example, using the equation above:

$$
\begin{array}{rr}
2 + x = & 10 \\
-2 \qquad & -2 \\
\hline
x = & 8
\end{array}
$$

Subtract 2 from each side.

Let's take a more difficult equation:

$$
\begin{array}{rcr}
3x + 12 = & x - 4 \\
-x \qquad & -x \\
\hline
2x + 12 = & -4 \\
-12 \qquad & -12 \\
\hline
2x \quad = & -16 \\
x \quad = & -8
\end{array}
$$

Subtract x from each side.

Subtract 12 from both sides.

Divide both sides by 2.

How do you know this is correct? To check your work, substitute –8 for x in the original equation: $3(-8) + 12 = -8 + (-4)$ or $-12 = -12$. Since both sides are the same, –8 was the correct answer.

Let's try an equation containing two fractions.

$$\frac{x}{20} = \frac{4}{16}$$

Related Skills: 24, 25, 26, 29, 32

Understand and Solve Equations

To solve this kind of equation, cross multiply.

$$16(x) = 20(4)$$
$$16x = 80$$
$$x = 5$$

Multiplying Expressions. To multiply two expressions such as $(x + 4)(x + 5)$, you multiply each term in one expression by each term in the other. Look at this example:

$$
\begin{array}{r}
x + 4 \\
x + 5 \\
\hline
5x + 20 \\
x^2 + 4x \\
\hline
x^2 + 9x + 20
\end{array}
$$

Be careful to account for any minus signs. Note what happens in the problem above if we change the second expression, $x + 5$, to $x - 5$:

$$
\begin{array}{r}
x + 4 \\
x - 5 \\
\hline
-5x - 20 \\
x^2 + 4x \\
\hline
x^2 - x - 20
\end{array}
$$

Dividing Expressions. Dividing expressions is a little tougher. Here is an example. Note that you take each expression in the numerator and divide it by the denominator.

$$\frac{6x^2 + 4x}{2x} = \frac{6x^2}{2x} + \frac{4x}{2x} = 3x + 2$$

Factoring Expressions. An ASVAB question might ask you to find the factors of an expression. The *factors* of a given expression are simpler expressions that, when multiplied together, produce that given expression. For example, when $(x + 4)$ and $(x + 5)$ are multiplied together, they produce the expression $x^2 + 9x + 20$. So $(x + 4)$ and $(x + 5)$ are factors of that more complex expression.

Factoring expressions can be asked in different ways. For example, you may be asked, "What two expressions can be multiplied by each other to get $x^2 + 15x + 36$?" Or you may be asked, "What are the factors of $x^2 + 15x + 36$?"

To solve these problems, think about the numbers. The final term in the expression is 36. What two numbers when multiplied together produce 36? Some possibilities are 6 and 6, or 3 and 12, or 18 and 2. The middle term of the expression is $15x$. Of the possible combinations you just identified, which two numbers when added together produce 15? The only possibilities are 3 and 12. So the factors of $x^2 + 15x + 36$ must be $(x + 3)$ and $(x + 12)$.

Graphing Equations. On the ASVAB you may be asked to choose which graph was produced from a given equation with two unknowns, such as $x = y + 3$. Note that many different pairs of numbers could be substituted for x and y in that equation and the equation would still be true. The graph of an equation like this shows all those different number pairs by their locations on the graph's x and y axes. A line linking those locations will be straight or curved depending on the equation.

When asked about graphing an equation, start by identifying pairs of numbers that can be substituted for the unknowns in the equation. It usually helps to make a chart like the one shown below:

If y is:	x must be:
0	3
1	4
2	5
−1	2
−2	1

Take those number pairs and plot them on a graph, remembering that the horizontal axis is the x axis and the vertical axis is the y axis. The numbers from the chart above have been plotted onto the graph below.

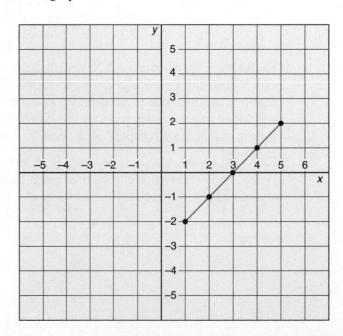

Understand and Solve Equations

Test Yourself!

Solve for x:

1 $5x + 10 = 35$ $\qquad$ $x =$ _____

2 $7x + 3 = 52$ $\qquad$ $x =$ _____

3 $\dfrac{50}{2x} = \dfrac{20}{24}$ $\qquad$ $x =$ _____

Solve for y:

4 $\dfrac{x}{y} = \dfrac{3}{4}$ $\qquad$ $y =$ _____

5 $12y - 3y = 24 + 3y$ $\qquad$ $y =$ _____

6 Solve for k: $\dfrac{j}{k} = \dfrac{l}{m}$ $\qquad$ $k =$ _____

7 Multiply: $(x + 3)(x + 7)$ $\qquad$ $=$ _____

8 Multiply: $(j + 6)(j - 2)$ $\qquad$ $=$ _____

9 Find the factors of $c^2 + 8c - 20$ _____

10 Find the factors of $g^2 - 6g - 16$ _____

Calculating Simple and Compound Interest

When you borrow money from a bank or take out a mortgage or a car loan, you have to pay interest. When you put money in a savings account or an interest-bearing checking account, you earn interest on it for as long as the money stays in the account. There are two basic kinds of interest, simple and compound.

Simple Interest. Let's say you borrow $10,000 to purchase a used car. The bank lends you that money (called the *principal*), but says that in order to have it, you must pay 5% interest on that principal sum every year.

You want to know how much interest you will have to pay on that original $10,000 in year 1 of your loan if you don't pay back any part of the principal. This kind of interest, calculated only on the principal, is called *simple interest*. You calculate simple interest using this formula:

$$Interest = Principal \times Rate \times Time$$

In this example, interest = $10,000 × 5% × 1 year. Calculate: $10,000 × 0.05 × 1 = $500. So you would owe $500 in interest for year 1. If you paid off the loan at the end of that year, you would have to pay a total of $10,500.

Here is another example. Suppose you put $5,000 in a savings account at 3% annual interest. How much would you have after 1 year?

$$Interest = Principal \times Rate \times Time$$

Interest = $5,000 × 0.03 × 1 = $150, so after one year your account would be worth $5,000 + $150 = $5,150.

On the ASVAB, you might get a problem that is not so straightforward. Perhaps you will be asked to calculate the rate of interest rather than the amount. Here is an example. On January 1 you put $6,000 in an interest-bearing savings account. On December 31 of that year, your balance was $6,120. What was the rate of interest?

The amount of interest you earned was $6,120 – $6,000 (the principal) = $120.

$$Interest = Principal \times Rate \times Time$$

Interest/Principal = Rate × Time   Divide both sides by principal

$120/$6,000 = 0.02 × 1 or 2%   The rate of interest = 2%.

Related Skills: 24, 25, 29, 32

Calculating Simple and Compound Interest

Compound Interest. Unlike simple interest, compound interest is calculated on the sum of the principal and any interest already earned. This sum increases ("compounds") regularly as more interest is added. You calculate compound interest using the same formula, but you apply the rate of interest to the new total every time the sum increases.

Here is an example. Suppose you put $5,000 in a fund that earns you 5% interest compounded annually. What would your balance be at the end of 3 years?

Year 1: $5,000 × 0.05 × 1 = $250 (interest earned)   End-of-Year Balance = $5,250

Year 2: $5,250 × 0.05 × 1 = $262.50 (interest earned)   End-of-Year Balance = $5,512.50

Year 3: $5,512.50 × 0.05 × 1 = $275.63 (interest earned)   End-of-Year Balance = $5,788.13

Test Yourself!

❶ You place $1,500 in an interest-bearing checking account that earns 2.5% annual interest. What will your balance be at the end of 1 year?

❷ You place $2,200 in an account that earns 3% interest compounded annually. How much will your balance be at the end of 4 years?

❸ You place $2,200 in an account that earns 3% interest compounded annually. If you are saving for a computer that costs $2,500, at the end of what year would you have enough money in this account?

Use Ratio and Proportion to Solve Problems

You will find this next skill very useful in solving the word problems on the ASVAB. This skill helps you think through and organize a problem, and then solve it!

Many word problems involving relationships between given quantities can be solved using ratios. A *ratio* is a relationship between two quantities such as "2 to 1" that stays true even when both quantities are multiplied or divided by the same amount. Two or more ratios with the same relationship form a *proportion*. For example, the ratio "2 to 1" is equal to the ratio "6 to 3." Therefore, $\frac{2}{1} = \frac{6}{3}$ is a proportion.

Here is an example of a word problem that you can solve using proportions. Suppose you burn 590 calories per hour running on a treadmill. How many calories will you burn if you run 3.75 hours per week?

"590 calories per hour" is the ratio "590 to 1." What would be the proportional ratio for 3.75 hours? Set up the problem like this:

$$\frac{590 \text{ calories}}{1 \text{ hour}} = \frac{x \text{ calories}}{3.75 \text{ hours}}$$

Cross multiply: $1x$ (or just x) $= 590 \times 3.75 = 2{,}212.5$ calories.

Here are two more word problems:

1. It takes 15 minutes to fill your bathtub with 56 gallons of water. How many gallons will be in the tub after 10 minutes?

   Set up the problem as proportional ratios:

   $$\frac{15 \text{ minutes}}{56 \text{ gallons}} = \frac{10 \text{ minutes}}{x \text{ gallons}}$$

   Cross multiply: $15x = 10 \times 56 = 560$
   $$x = 37.33 \text{ gallons}$$

2. Your car's gas tank holds 22 gallons of fuel. It takes 130 seconds to fill the tank. How long will it take to pump 17 gallons of fuel into the tank?

   $$\frac{22 \text{ gallons}}{130 \text{ seconds}} = \frac{17 \text{ gallons}}{x \text{ seconds}}$$

   $22x = 2{,}210$
   $$x = 100.45 \text{ seconds}$$

Related Skills: 24, 25, 29, 32, 38

Use Ratio and Proportion to Solve Problems

Test Yourself!

1. A "super burger" has 850 calories, and 3,500 calories equal 1 pound. How many pounds does Gene gain by eating one super burger?

   _____

2. Sal runs at a rate that burns 350 calories per hour. How many calories will Sal burn if he runs 4.2 hours per week for 2 weeks?

   _____

3. A team can pack 34 boxes of books every 3 minutes. How many boxes can be packed in 2 hours?

   _____

4. Lakeisha wants to travel from Chicago to Denver by train. The train travels at 105 miles per hour and Denver is 1,190 miles away. How many hours will it take Lakeisha to reach her destination?

   _____

5. If Jay can pack 14 crates of oranges in 1 hour, how many crates can he pack in an 8-hour day with an hour for lunch and two 15-minute breaks?

   _____

6. If together Tom and Tyree can lay 250 square feet of carpet in 1.5 hours, how many square feet can they lay in 6 hours?

   _____

Calculate Distance, Rate, and Time

It is very helpful to be able to calculate how much time it will take to get from one place to another when traveling at a certain speed, or how far you will travel if you are moving at a certain rate or speed for a given amount of time

You might find questions like these on the ASVAB. They are not difficult to solve. The formula to use is

$$distance = rate \times time$$
$$d = r \times t$$

Distance is how far you travel, *rate* is how fast you are moving, and *time* is how long it takes you to travel.

Let's work through a few examples.

Find the Distance. If you travel on your motorcycle at an average speed of 45 miles per hour for 2 hours, how far will you travel?

Set up the information in the formula:

$$d = \frac{45\ mi}{hr} \times \frac{2\ hrs}{1} = 90 \text{ miles}$$

Find the Rate. You are traveling to visit your aunt who lives 350 miles away. You want to arrive at her home 6 hours from now. At what average speed must you travel?

Set up the problem information using the formula $d = r \times t$.

350 miles = $r \times 6$ hours; solve for the unknown r: $\frac{350\ mi}{6\ hrs} = r$

Divide 350 by 6 to get 58.33 = 58.33 miles/hour, or about 58 miles/hour

Find the Time. Suppose the problem gives you the distance and the rate, but you have to calculate the travel time. Here is an example:

Sanjay walks 4 miles every day at an average rate of 4.5 miles per hour. How long does it take him to walk that distance?

Set up the problem information using the formula $d = r \times t$.

$4\ mi = \frac{4.5\ mi}{hr} \times t$; $t = 4 \div 4.5 = 0.888$ hour or 0.89 hour

Suppose you are asked for that in minutes. You would calculate as follows: 1 hour = 60 minutes; 0.89 × 60 = 53.4 minutes.

Watch the units that you are given in the problem, and be sure you give the answer in the units requested!

Related Skills: 29, 32, 39, 40

Calculate Distance, Rate, and Time

Test Yourself!

Solve the following problems.

❶ Dexter is on a train from Denver to Chicago. The train travels an average of 125 miles per hour. The trip takes 8.75 hours. What is the distance between those two cities?

_____

❷ Kim rides his motorcycle to visit a friend who lives 68 miles away. He travels at an average speed of 45 miles/hour. How long does it take him to make the trip?

_____

❸ A rocket is traveling from Earth to the moon. If the distance to the moon is 384,403 km and the rocket takes 5 days to get there, at what average speed is the rocket traveling per day? Per hour?

_____

❹ Jake and Joan traveled on their motorcycles the distance from Des Moines, IA to Mobile, AL. They have traveled 14 hours at an average rate of 45 miles/hour. How far did they travel?

_____

❺ Paul and a dozen of his friends in the Edgemont Cycling Club are cycling across the United States to raise awareness of how healthy cycling is for fitness and how good it is for the environment. They started on the west coast and completed their 2,790 mile journey in 55 days. On an average, what was their mileage each day?

_____

Determining Change and Percent Change

On the ASVAB, you will probably encounter questions that ask you to find the percent something has changed from what it was before, or the actual amount something has changed if it has increased or decreased by a given percent. For example, you may be asked how much more money you will make if you receive a 7% salary increase, or what the new price of an item is after a 10% markdown from its original price.

The only difficulty with these problems is learning how to set them up correctly. Once you set them up, the calculations are easy.

Finding the Percent of Change. Here is an example of a problem that gives you the actual amount of change and asks you to find the percent of change.

José works part-time at an electronics store and earns $400 per month. Since José is an excellent worker, his boss tells him that starting next month his salary will increase to $475 per month. By what percent will José's monthly salary increase?

Set up the problem like this:

$$Percent\ Change = \frac{amount\ of\ change}{starting\ point}$$

$$Percent\ Change = \frac{475-400}{400} = \frac{75}{400} = 0.1875\ \text{ or } 19\%$$

Finding the Amount of Change. Here is an example of a problem that gives you the percent of change and asks you to find the actual amount of change.

Tamara wants to purchase a computer. At her favorite store, she sees one selling for $2,000. The store clerk tells her that next month the computer will be on sale at a 15% discount. How much will the computer cost at the discount price?

Use the formula $Percent\ Change = \dfrac{amount\ of\ change}{starting\ point}$. Substitute the numbers given in the problem.

$$15\% = \frac{x}{\$2,000} = 0.15 \times 2,000 = \$300.$$

$300 is the amount by which the price will decrease. But the problem asks for the new price, not the amount of change. So subtract $300 from the original $2,000 price. The discount price is $1,700.

Related Skills: 23, 24, 25, 27, 31, 32, 33, 38, 39, 40

Determining Change and Percent Change

Test Yourself!

Solve the following problems.

1 Ned measured 55 inches tall at age 13 and 69 inches tall at age 17. What was his percent change in height over that period of time?

_____

2 The temperature on January 1 was 54 degrees; on January 2 the temperature plummeted by 25%. What was the temperature on January 2?

_____

3 An advertisement says, "If you place your order today, you can purchase the toolkit for $35. But if you wait until tomorrow, the price will increase by 55%." What will the toolkit cost if you wait until tomorrow to place your order?

_____

4 In 2010, the local hospital federation reported that charitable contributions to the local hospital were $2,500,000. The members of the foundation want to increase their contributions in 3 years by $500,000. What percent increase is their goal?

_____

5 The local electronics store marked down an HD television by 30%. If the original cost was $1700, how much is the sale price?

_____

6 In a 5-year time period, the oak tree that Yasir planted in his front yard, grew by 40% in height. If the tree started at 25 ft, what was the height after 5 years?

_____

Calculate the Probability of an Event

Probability is a way of calculating the likelihood that a certain event will happen. For instance, when you roll a six-sided die, a probability calculation will tell you how likely you are to roll a 6. Or suppose you have a jar containing four red marbles and six blue marbles. A probability calculation will tell you how likely you are to draw a red marble from the jar on your first try without looking. On the ASVAB, you may encounter questions that ask you to calculate a probability.

To calculate probability, first consider that in situations like the ones just mentioned, many different things could happen. In math, each one is called an *outcome*. When rolling a six-sided die, there are six possible outcomes: you could roll a 1, 2, 3, 4, 5, or 6. When drawing a marble at random from a jar containing 10 marbles, you could draw any one of the marbles, so there are 10 possible outcomes. In both cases, all of these possible outcomes are equally likely.

However, in both cases you want to know the likelihood of a particular outcome: rolling a 6 or drawing a red marble. You can call this a *positive outcome*. Because there is only one 6 on the die, and only four red marbles in the jar, it is not equally likely that you will or won't roll a 6 or draw a red marble.

To calculate probability, use the following formula:

$$\text{Probability} = \frac{\text{number of positive outcomes}}{\text{number of possible outcomes}}$$

For the die, there are six possible outcomes (rolling a 1, 2, 3, 4, 5, or 6) but only one positive outcome (rolling a 6). Substitute these numbers into the formula:

$$\text{Probability} = \frac{1}{6} = 0.1666 \text{ or } 0.17.$$

The probability of rolling a 6 is about 17%.

For the marbles in a jar, there are 10 marbles so there are 10 possible outcomes. But there are only four red marbles, so only four possible positive outcomes. Substitute these numbers into the formula:

$$\text{Probability} = \frac{4}{10} = 0.4.$$

The probability of drawing a red marble is 40%.

Let's try a more difficult example. You have 120 coins in a jar. They are divided as follows:

Pennies	33
Nickels	23
Dimes	29
Quarters	15
$\frac{1}{2}$ dollars	20

Related Skills: 23, 24, 25, 27, 29, 32, 33, 40

Calculate the Probability of an Event

What is the probability of selecting a quarter at random on the first draw? There are 120 coins, so there are 120 possible outcomes. There are 15 quarters, so there are 15 possible positive outcomes. Substitute these numbers into the formula:

$$\text{Probability} = \frac{15}{120} = 0.125 \text{ or } 12.5\%$$

Test Yourself!

Solve the following problems.

1 Dana has a very large collection of music CDs. She has classified the CDs by type of music, and the results are shown in the following table.

Rock	245
Classical	111
Country	345
Metal	189
Jazz	53
Rap	57

The CDs are arranged completely randomly in a cabinet. If Dana reaches into the cabinet without looking and pulls out a CD, what is the probability that the CD will be either Rock or Country?

_____

2 Based on the information in the table above, what is the probability that the first CD that Dana pulls from the cabinet without looking will NOT be Jazz or Rap?

_____

3 On a game show, you can spin a wheel to win $100, $1000, $5000, $10,000, $25,000, $50,000, $100,000, or $250,000. Each prize occupies a single space on the wheel, and all the spaces are identical in size. What is the probability that the wheel will stop on $50,000 or $25,000?

_____

Analyze Lines and Angles

ASVAB math tests include some questions on geometry. Often these questions will ask you to analyze lines and angles. This takes a little knowledge and some common sense. An angle is really two lines (sometimes called *rays*) that meet up at the same point. Angles are measured in degrees (°). Here are a few examples:

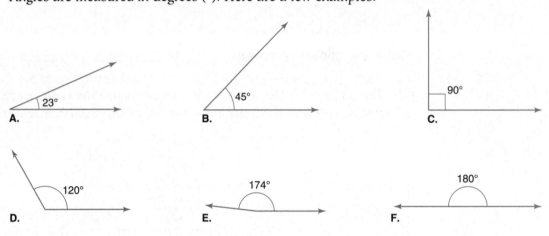

- Angles that measure less than 90° are called *acute angles*. Figures A and B show acute angles.
- Angles that measure greater than 90° are called *obtuse angles*. Figures D and E show obtuse angles.
- A *right angle* measures exactly 90°. Figure C shows a right angle. A right angle is often indicated by the insertion of a small square as shown in Figure C.
- A *straight angle* measures 180°. It is a straight line. Figure F shows a straight angle.
- If you keep increasing the size of an angle, you eventually get a circle, which measures 360°.

Angles are frequently combined, as shown in Figures G and H.

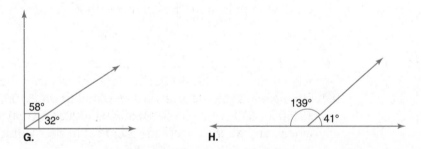

In Figure G, two acute angles are combined to create a 90° right angle. Any two or more acute angles that add up to 90° are called *complementary angles*.

In Figure H, two angles are combined to create a straight angle (straight line) of 180°. Any two or more angles that add up to 180° are called *supplementary angles*.

Related Skill: 23

Analyze Lines and Angles

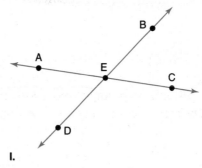

I.

Figure I shows two lines that cross each other to form four angles. Angles can be named by points on the lines composing them. So the four angles are named ∠AEB, ∠BEC, ∠CED, and ∠DEA. (The symbol "∠" means "angle.") When two straight lines cross as shown, the angles that are opposite each other are equal in measure. In the figure:

$$∠DEA = ∠BEC$$
$$∠AEB = ∠CED$$

Note that the pairs of adjoining angles are supplementary:

$$∠BEC + ∠CED = 180° \qquad ∠DEA + ∠AEB = 180°$$
$$∠CED + ∠DEA = 180° \qquad ∠AEB + ∠BEC = 180°$$

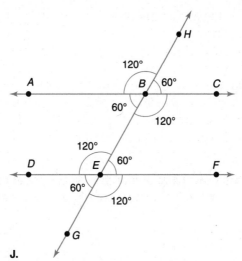

J.

Figure J shows two parallel straight lines *AC* and *DF*. They are crossed by a third straight line *GH*. This arrangement creates several pairs of equal angles (in this case, the pairs are 60° and 120°). Two pairs are called *alternate interior angles*. They are:

$$∠ABE = ∠BEF = 60°$$
$$∠DEB = ∠EBC = 120°$$

There are also two pairs of equal *alternate exterior angles*. They are:

$$∠ABH = ∠GEF = 120°$$
$$∠HBC = ∠DEG = 60°$$

Pay close attention to these angle pairs! You are almost certain to see a question about them on the ASVAB.

Analyze Lines and Angles

Test Yourself!

Solve the following problems.

1 If ∠ABC is a right angle and ∠ABD measures 22°, what is the measure of angle ∠DBC?

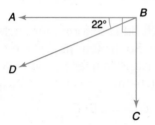

Answer: _____

_____

2 If ABC is a straight line and ∠CBD measures 52°, what is the measure of ∠ABD?

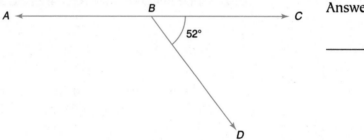

Answer: _____

_____

3 The figure below shows two straight lines crossing each other. If ∠CBD measures 73°, what is the measure of ∠ABE? What is the measure of ∠ABC?

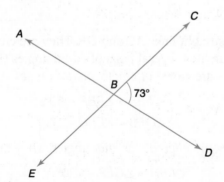

Answer: _____

_____

Related Skill: 23

Analyze Lines and Angles

④ If *LMG* and *YMJ* are straight lines and ∠*LMP* measures 40°, what is the measure of ∠*JMG*?

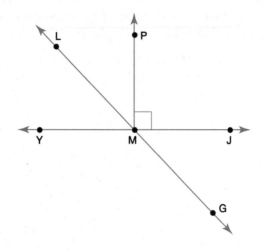

Answer: _____

_____

Questions 5–8 are based on the following diagram. Lines ABD and EFG are parallel.

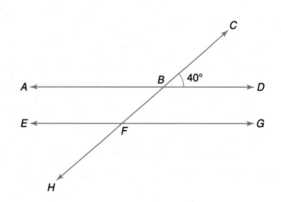

⑤ If ∠*CBD* = 40°, what is the measure of ∠*ABC*? _____

⑥ If ∠*CBD* = 40°, what is the measure of ∠*DBF*? _____

⑦ If ∠*CBD* = 40º, what is the measure of ∠*ABF*? _____

⑧ If ∠*CBD* = 40º, what is the measure of ∠*EFH*? _____

Understand the Characteristics of Triangles

A triangle is a figure with three sides and three interior angles. The ASVAB often includes questions about triangles. To answer these questions, you need to be familiar with some characteristics of these geometric figures.

The three interior angles in a triangle always add up to 180°. So in Fig. 1, if ∠CAB measures 20°, the other two angles must add up to 160°.

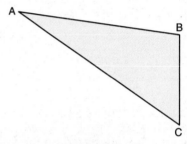

Figure 1.

Right Triangles. A right triangle is a triangle in which one of the angles measures 90°. Figure 2 shows a right triangle. Because the sum of the three angles must be 180°, the two angles in a right triangle that are *not* right angles must add up to 90°.

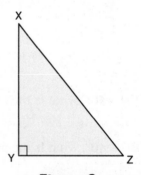

Figure 2.

In the figure, ∠XYZ measures 90°. Therefore, ∠YXZ and ∠YZX must add up to 90°. If you were told that that ∠YXZ = 40°, then ∠YZX must measure 90 − 40 = 50°.

Related Skills: 23, 24, 25, 34, 38, 44

Understand the Characteristics of Triangles

Equilateral Triangles. In an equilateral triangle, all three sides are equal in length. All three interior three angles are also equal. Each one measures 60°. Figure 3 shows an equilateral triangle.

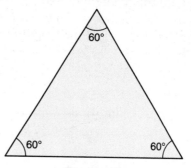

Figure 3.

Isosceles Triangles. An isosceles triangle has at least two equal interior angles and two equal sides. Figure 4 shows an isosceles triangle. In this triangle, $\angle KJL = \angle KLJ$. If $\angle KJL$ measures 65°, then $\angle KLJ$ must also measure 65°. Often an ASVAB question will ask you the measure of the remaining angle in an isosceles triangle. In this case, $\angle JKL$ measures 180° − (65° + 65°) = 50°

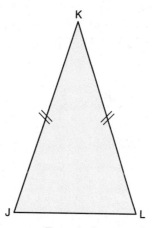

Figure 4.

Largest Angles and Longest Sides. In triangles, the side opposite the largest angle is always the longest side. So in Fig. 1 above, the side opposite $\angle ABC$ (side AC) is the longest side. In Fig. 2, the side opposite $\angle XYZ$ (side XZ) is the longest side. In Fig. 3, because all three angles are equal, all three sides are equal in length.

Understand the Characteristics of Triangles

Pythagorean Theorem. The Pythagorean Theorem is a rule that applies to right triangles. The theorem states that the lengths of the sides of a right triangle relate to one another according to the formula $a^2 + b^2 = c^2$. Each letter in the theorem represents the length of a side. So if you know the lengths of two sides of a right triangle, you can always use the theorem to find the length of the third side. For example, in the right triangle shown below, if you know that side a = 3 inches and side b = 4 inches, you can use the theorem to find the length of side c.

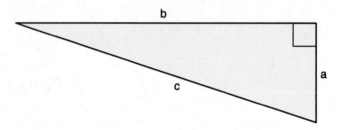

Substitute the numbers into the formula:

$3^2 + 4^2 = c^2$

$9 + 16 = 25$, so side c is the square root of 25 or 5 inches.

Understand the Characteristics of Triangles

Test Yourself!

1 In the triangle below, if ∠y measures 25° and ∠z measures 50°, which side is the longest side?

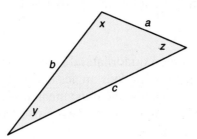

Answer: _____

_____

2 The figure below shows an isosceles triangle. If ∠a measures 30°, what is the measure of ∠b?

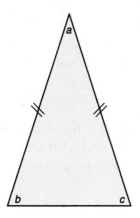

Answer: _____

_____

3 In the figure below, if side a = 7 cm and side b = 9 cm, what is the length of side c?

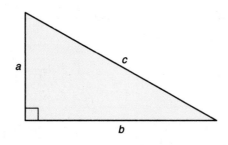

Answer: _____

_____

Know the Characteristics of Quadrilaterals

The prefix *quad-* means "four," so quadrilaterals are four-sided figures. ASVAB geometry questions frequently involve quadrilaterals and their characteristics, so you want to be familiar with them beforehand.

All quadrilaterals have four sides and four interior angles. The four interior angles always add up to 360°.

Squares. Perhaps the most common quadrilateral is the square. In a square, all four sides are equal in length, and each of the four angles is equal in measure. So if the total measure of all four angles is 360°, each angle must measure exactly 90°. If one side of a square is length x, then each of the other three sides is also length x.

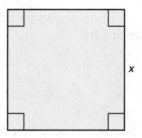

Rectangles. A rectangle is a quadrilateral that has two pairs of sides of equal length. The figure below shows a rectangle. In the figure, the two longer sides are the same length and the two shorter sides are the same length. Each interior angle measures 90°. The total of all the angles is 360°.

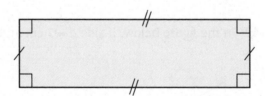

Related Skills: 23, 24, 25, 44, 45

Know the Characteristics of Quadrilaterals

Rhombuses. If you took a square and pushed it over slightly, you would create a rhombus. In a rhombus, all four sides are equal, but the interior angles are not all equal. Instead, each angle is equal to the one opposite it, but not to the others. Also, in a rhombus the opposite sides are parallel to each other. The figure below shows a rhombus. In the figure, angles a and c are equal and angles b and d are equal. Note the dotted line that runs diagonally through the figure. It splits the rhombus into two triangles, and it also splits the two corner angles into two equal parts. As in every other quadrilateral, the interior angles in a rhombus add up to 360°. In the triangles created by the dotted line (as in all other triangles), the interior angles add up to 180°.

Suppose you are told that angles a and c each measure 60°. If the dotted line splits each one into two equal parts, then angles a^1, a^2, c^1, and c^2 must each measure 30°. And because the interior angles of a triangle add up to 180°, then angle b must measure $180 - (30 + 30) = 120°$.

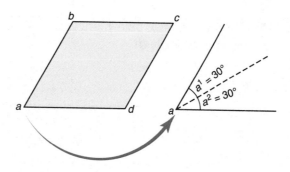

Parallelograms. If a rhombus is "a square pushed over," then a parallelogram is "a rectangle pushed over." A parallelogram has two pairs of equal sides and two pairs of equal angles. The equal sides are parallel to each other. The figure below shows a parallelogram. Angles a and c are equal and angles b and d are equal.

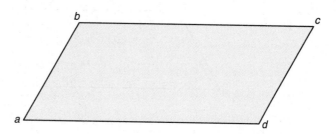

Trapezoids. A trapezoid is a quadrilateral with two parallel sides and two sides that are not parallel. The figure below shows a trapezoid. The two longer sides in this trapezoid are parallel.

Test Yourself!

❶ If in the rectangle below, angle *a* and angle *c* are equal in measure. What is the measure of angle *d*?

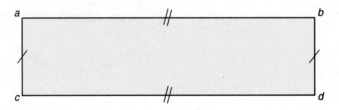

Answer: _____

❷ In the parallelogram below, angle *a* = 34°. What is the measure of angle *b*?

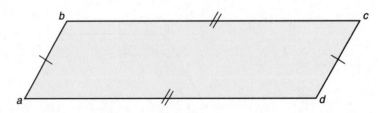

Answer: _____

Related Skills: 23, 24, 25, 44, 45

3 In the trapezoid below, which two sides are parallel?

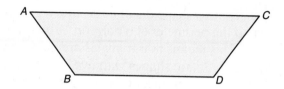

Ⓐ AB and BD
Ⓑ AB and CD
Ⓒ AC and BD
Ⓓ AC and CD

4 In the trapezoid below, if ∠a = 55°, how large is ∠b?

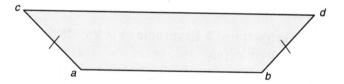

Answer: _____

5 In the square below, if ∠a + ∠b = 180°. What is the size of ∠c?

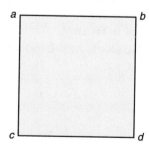

Answer: _____

Calculate the Perimeter of Polygons

The *perimeter* is the distance around a given shape. On the ASVAB, you may be asked to find the perimeter of a polygon. A *polygon* is any shape with three or more straight sides. This means that triangles are polygons. Squares and other quadrilaterals are also polygons. So are shapes with five, six, or more straight sides. It is usually easy to calculate the perimeter of a polygon. All you have to do is add up the lengths of the sides. When two or more sides are equal in length, you can use multiplication.

Perimeter of a Square or a Rhombus. If the length of one side of a square is 6 feet, then the perimeter is 6 ft + 6 ft + 6 ft + 6 ft = 24 ft. Because the four sides of a square are equal, you can also multiply the length of one side by 4. In mathematical "shorthand," the formula for the perimeter of a square is $P = 4s$ where s is the length of one side. A rhombus also has four equal sides, so you can use the same formula to find the perimeter. If each side of a rhombus measures 3 cm, the perimeter is 4×3 cm = 12 cm.

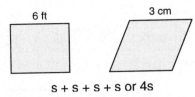

s + s + s + s or 4s

Perimeter of a Rectangle or a Parallelogram. To find the perimeter of a rectangle or a parallelogram, once again you add up the lengths of the four sides. Each of these figures has two parallel long sides (the length, or *l*) and two parallel short sides (the width, or *w*). So if the length is 24 in and the width is 12 in, then the perimeter = 24 in + 24 in + 12 in + 12 in = 72 in.

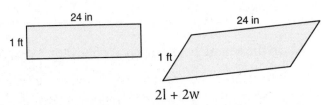

2l + 2w

Perimeter of a Triangle. To find the perimeter of a triangle, once again add up the lengths of the sides. In the triangle below, the perimeter is 11 m.

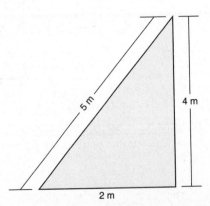

Tip

Sometimes on the ASVAB the measurements may be shown in different units. For example, the length might be 24 in and the width might be 1 ft. Be sure that all measurements are in the same units before calculating the perimeter, and be sure your answer is in the units asked for in the question.

Related Skills: 23, 24, 26, 29, 31, 32, 45, 46

Calculate the Perimeter of Polygons

If the question states that a triangle is an equilateral triangle, all three sides are the same length. If it is an isosceles triangle, you know that there are at least two equal sides. In the equilateral triangle below, if one side measures 37 in, the perimeter is 3 × 37 in = 111 in. In the isosceles triangle with the measurements shown, the perimeter is (2 × 14 cm) + 3 cm = 31 cm.

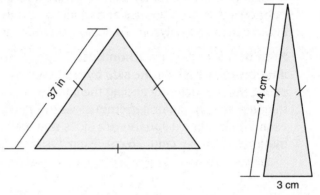

Perimeter of Other Polygons. For any shape with straight sides, you can find the perimeter by adding up the lengths of the sides. In the five-sided shape below, the perimeter is 48 + 48 + 10 + 12 + 54 = 172 in. Don't forget to pay attention to the units.

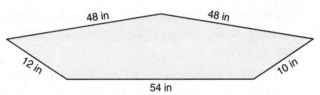

Test Yourself!

❶ Paul and Paula are planning a flower garden in their back yard. The garden will have a fence all around its edge. If the shape of the garden is a parallelogram with long sides each measuring 4.3 m and short sides each measuring 1.7 m, how many meters of fencing should they purchase?

_____

If each meter of fencing costs $10, how much will the fence cost?

_____

❷ Chuck is putting baseboard around the edges of his living room floor. His living room is a rectangle measuring 10 ft by 13 ft 6 in. How many inches of baseboard does he have to purchase? Remember: 12 inches = 1 ft.

_____

Area is how many square units of space are enclosed by the sides of a flat shape. Think of a carpet that takes up a certain amount of space. A room-sized carpet covers more square units of space than a small rug. There are formulas for calculating the area of regular polygon shapes like squares and triangles. On the ASVAB, you are likely to be asked to find the area of a polygon. To do so, you need to memorize a few basic formulas.

Area of a Square or a Rhombus. It is easy to find the area of these polygons. Simply multiply the length of one side by the length of any other side. Because all the sides are equal, you are actually finding the square of one side. So here is the formula for finding the area of a square or a rhombus: area = s^2 where s is the length of one side. For example, imagine a square with sides that each measure 6 cm. To calculate the area, multiply: 6 cm × 6 cm = 36 cm² ("cm²" is read "square centimeters").

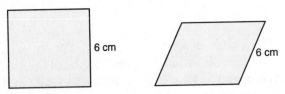

Always remember that area is indicated in square "units." The units can be square meters, square miles, square yards, square centimeters, or whatever unit the problem asks for.

Area of a Rectangle or a Parallelogram. To find the area of these shapes, use this formula: area = length × width (also expressed as $l \times w$). In the rectangle and parallelogram below, the area is 90 inches × 20 inches =1,800 square inches or 1,800 in².

Area of a Triangle. Triangles get a bit more complicated. To find the area of a triangle, use this formula: area = $\frac{1}{2}$ base × height (also expressed as $\frac{1}{2}$ bh). The base is the bottom of the triangle. The height is a vertical line from the top of the triangle to the base. Often this line is shown as a dashed line, as in the figure below. (On the ASVAB, if you are asked to find the area of a triangle, the height measurement will be given to you, either in the problem or in a figure.) Look at the triangle below. The base measures 25 ft. The dashed line from the top to the base measures 20 ft. Substitute these numbers into the formula: $\frac{1}{2}$ (25 × 20) = $\frac{1}{2}$ (500) = 250 ft².

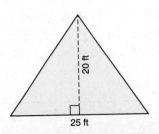

Related Skills: 23, 24, 25, 28, 29, 30, 31, 32, 44, 45, 46, 47

Calculate the Area of Polygons

Area of a Parallelogram. Now let's step it up a notch and work with parallelograms. If you think about it, a parallelogram is made up of two triangles. See the figure below.

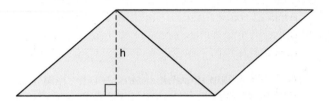

To calculate the area of a parallelogram, use this formula: $2 \times (\frac{1}{2}$ base $\times$ height) or simply base $\times$ height (bh). The trick is to identify the base and the height. Look at the triangle on the left (the one with a top that points upward). Its base is the base of the parallelogram. Then draw a line from the top of that triangle down to the base. That line is the height of the parallelogram. (On the ASVAB, if you need to find the area of a parallelogram, you will be given the measurements of these lines.)

Area of a Trapezoid. Finding the area of a trapezoid is a bit more difficult, but not impossible.

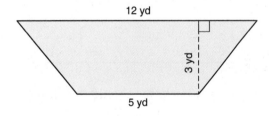

To find the area of a trapezoid, use this formula: $\frac{1}{2}$(base$_1$ + base$_2$) $\times$ height. To calculate, look for the length measure of each of the bases. Then draw the height, which is a line from one of the angles to the opposite base. (On the ASVAB, if you are asked to find the area of a trapezoid, you will be given the height measurement.)

Substitute the measurements from the figure into the formula: base$_1$ = 12 yd, base$_2$ = 5 yd, and the height = 3 yd. So area = $\frac{1}{2}$(12 + 5) $\times$ 3 = 8.5 $\times$ 3 = 25.5 yd^2 or 26 yd^2.

Calculate the Area of Polygons

Test Yourself!

1 Jamal wants to paint a wall in his kitchen. The wall measures 12 ft × 20 ft. What is the area of the wall?

_____

If a gallon of paint covers 200 ft^2, how many gallons of paint will he use?

_____

2 Tom and Lee need to purchase grass seed for their yard. The yard is the shape of a triangle with a base of 18 m and a height of 12 m. What is the area of the yard?

_____

If grass seed comes in 1 lb packages, and 1 lb is recommended for every 10 m^2, how many pounds will they need?

_____

How many packages should they buy?

_____

3 A patio measures 10 ft × 15 ft. What is the area of the patio?

_____

4 Sammy cuts grass in a neighbor's yard. The yard is in the shape of a parallelogram and has a height of 56 m and a base of 16 m. What is the area of the yard?

_____

Related Skills: 23, 24, 25, 28, 29, 30, 31, 32, 44, 45, 46, 47

Calculate the Area of Polygons

5 Sammy is cutting the grass in the yard described in the previous question, if he can cut all the grass in 4 hours, how many square meters can he cut in 1 hour?

_____

6 Sally tiled the floor of her kitchen. The rectangular kitchen measures 14 ft × 28 ft. What is the area of the kitchen floor?

_____

7 Given the information in Question 6, if Sally took 4 hours to tile the kitchen floor, how many square feet could she tile in 1 hour?

_____

8 Gina is planting a garden in the shape of a triangle. The height is 4 m and the base is 16 m. What it the area of the garden?

_____

9 Given the information in Question 8, if Gina can plant 6 tomato plants in every square meter of space, how many tomato plants can she plant?

_____

10 If a table top measures 5 ft × 6 ft, what is the area?

_____

11 Given the information in question 10, if Susan purchases a table cloth to cover the table top and to have the cloth hanging over 1 ft on each side, how many square meters must the table cloth be?

_____

Calculate the Volume and Surface Area of Solids

You have reviewed *area*, which is the amount of space enclosed by the sides of a flat (two-dimensional) shape. The next step is to consider *volume*—the amount of space a solid object takes up in three dimensions.

A square has two dimensions, length and width. But if you add the third dimension of height (sometimes called depth), the square becomes a cube, as shown in the figure below. While a square has only one side, a cube has six sides with equal areas and equal perimeters.

 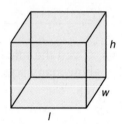

If you add the third dimension of height to a rectangle, it becomes a solid object called a *prism*, which looks like this:

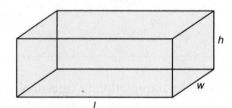

Volume of a Cube or a Prism. To calculate the volume of a cube or a prism, use this formula: length × width × height. So if a cube has a side of 15 cm, its volume is 15 cm × 15 cm × 15 cm = 3,375 cm³. ("cm³" is read "cubic centimeters." Note that volume is always expressed in cubic units.)

If a prism has a length of 3 ft, a width of 4 ft, and a height of 9 ft, its volume is 3 ft × 4 ft × 9 ft = 108 ft³.

Surface Area of Solids. Occasionally on the ASVAB you may be asked to calculate the surface area of a three-dimensional solid. In this case you need to calculate the area of each face of the solid, then add the areas together.

*   If you are asked to calculate the surface area of a cube, you can use this formula: Surface Area = 6*lw*
*   If you are asked to calculate the surface area of a rectangular prism, you can use this formula: Surface Area = 2(*lh*) + 2(*lw*) + 2(*wh*)

Calculate the Volume and Surface Area of Solids

Test Yourself!

1 Jamie has purchased a rectangular fish tank. It is 6 in wide, 18 in long, and 9 in high. What is the volume of the fish tank?

_____

If one gallon of water takes up 512 in^3 of space, how many gallons of water does Jamie need to fill his tank?

_____

2 By the gate to the football field there is a rectangular trash can that measures 1 yd high, 18 in wide, and 24 in long. What is the volume of the trash can?

_____

3 Books are packed in a cardboard box for shipping. The box is 9 in high, 11 in wide, and 24 in long. What is the volume of the box?

_____

4 Ebony is wrapping a gift. The gift is in a rectangular box which measures 6 cm × 8 cm × 12 cm. How much wrapping paper should she use if she wants to cover the box with exactly no paper left over?

_____

5 The freezer in a local fast food restaurant measures 10 ft high, 12 ft deep, and 8 ft wide. What is the storage capacity in cubic feet?

_____

Skill 50

Calculate the Measures of a Circle, a Sphere, or a Cylinder

On the ASVAB, often there are questions that ask you to find certain measures of a circle. You may even have to calculate the volume of a *sphere* (a round three-dimensional object) or a *cylinder* (a solid with circular surfaces on either end). The good news is that there are no sides to add up!

Let's start by defining some terms.

- The **radius** of a circle is the distance from the center to any point on the edge.
- The **diameter** of a circle is a straight line from one side of a circle to the opposite side, passing through the center. The diameter is twice the length of the radius.
- The **circumference** of a circle is the distance around its outside edge. The circumference is the perimeter of the circle.

Finding the Radius or Diameter of a Circle. Usually if you are asked to find the radius, you will be given the length of the diameter. Simply divide that length by 2. Similarly, if you are asked to find the diameter, you will usually be given the length of the radius. Simply multiply that length by 2.

Finding the Circumference of a Circle. This calculation is a little more complicated. As a multiplier, you need to use a number represented by the Greek letter π (spelled "pi" in English and pronounced "pie"). That number is approximately 3.14, and you can use that decimal number in your calculation. To find the circumference of a circle, use this formula: Circumference = πd where d is the diameter of the circle.

For example, for the circle shown which has a diameter of 4 cm, the circumference = 4 cm × 3.14 = 12.56 cm.

Finding the Area of a Circle. To find the area of a circle, use this formula: Area = πr^2 where r is the radius of the circle. So for a circle with a radius measuring 19 in, area = $3.14 \times (19)^2 = 3.14 \times 361 = 1133.54$ in². Remember that area is two-dimensional, so it must be expressed in square units.

Finding the Volume of a Sphere. A sphere is a round solid like a balloon or a basketball. The radius of a sphere is a line from the center of the sphere to any point on its outside surface, as shown in the figure below.

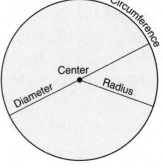

To calculate the volume of a sphere, use this formula:

Volume = $\left(\dfrac{4}{3}\right)\pi r^3$ where r is the radius of the sphere.

So if the radius of a sphere is 10 cm, its volume = $\dfrac{4}{3} \times 3.14 \times 10^3$.

Follow the order of operations you learned earlier: $\dfrac{4}{3} \times 3.14 \times 1000 = \dfrac{4}{3} \times 3,140 = 4,186.67$ cm³.

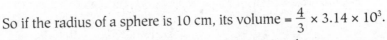

Related Skills: 23, 24, 25, 28, 29, 30, 31, 32, 44, 45, 46, 47, 48

Finding the Volume of a Cylinder. A cylinder is a solid object bounded on either end by a flat circular face. It is shaped like a pipe or a tube. When calculating volume, it helps to think of a cylinder as a series of identical circles placed one on top of another like pancakes. You can calculate the volume simply by multiplying the area of each circle times the height of the cylinder. Use this formula: Volume = $\pi r^2 h$ where r is the radius of any circle in the cylinder and h is the height of the cylinder.

For example, suppose the cylinder shown has a radius of 12 ft and a height of 45 ft. Its volume = $3.14 \times (12)^2 \times 45 = 3.14 \times 144 \times 45 = 20,347.2$ ft^3.

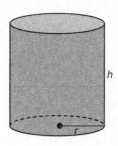

Test Yourself!

❶ Doug is racing his cycle on a circular track. The track has a radius of 0.25 miles. If Doug circles the track 4 times, how many miles will he travel?

_____

❷ Jenny and Jack are paving a circular patio. Its diameter is 14 ft. What is the area of the patio?

_____

❸ Blair intends to blow up 10 perfectly round balloons for her birthday party. If each balloon has a diameter of 8 in when fully inflated, what will be the total volume of all 10 balloons?

_____

❹ A potato chip can in the shape of a cylinder is 16 in high and has a top with a diameter of 4 in. What is the volume of the can?

_____

AFQT Posttest

The following 50 questions represent the 50 skills covered in this book. The first 22 questions check your reading, and the remaining 28 check your math knowledge.

For each question, circle the answer of your choice. At the end of the test, transfer your answers to the Scoring Sheet on page 160 to check your work.

Read the following passage and answer questions 1–5.

The Clear Skies project would protect public health and the environment by improving air quality, decreasing exposure to fine particles and ozone, and reducing deposition of sulfur, nitrogen, and mercury. Reductions in fine particle and ozone levels under Clear Skies would result in 7,800 fewer premature deaths and $55 billion in annual health and visibility benefits nationwide each year.

Under Clear Skies, each year, by 2020, Americans would experience approximately:

- 14,100 fewer premature deaths;
- 8,800 fewer cases of chronic bronchitis;
- 30,000 fewer hospitalizations/emergency room visits for cardiovascular and respiratory symptoms; and
- 12.5 million fewer days with respiratory illnesses and symptoms, including work loss days, restricted activity days, and school days.

The <u>monetized</u> benefits of the project would total approximately $113 billion annually by 2020, substantially outweighing the annual costs of $6.3 billion. This includes:

- $110 billion dollars in health benefits;
- $3 billion in benefits from improving visibility at select National Parks and Wilderness Areas.

This does not include the many additional benefits that cannot currently be quantified but are expected to be significant, including the health benefits associated with reduced exposure to mercury and ecological benefits associated with reductions in acid rain and coastal eutrophication.

❶ In this passage, the word <u>monetized</u> most nearly means

  Ⓐ healthy.
  Ⓑ wealthy.
  Ⓒ monetary.
  Ⓓ constructive.

❷ According to the passage, how many visits to the hospital would be saved if the Clear Skies project is successful?

  Ⓐ 7,800
  Ⓑ 55 billion
  Ⓒ 8,800
  Ⓓ 30,000

❸ In the passage, the prefix *pre-* in <u>premature</u> means which of the following?

  Ⓐ Behind
  Ⓑ Before
  Ⓒ After
  Ⓓ Since

AFQT Posttest

4 Which of the following is the main idea of the passage?

(A) This country needs to stop polluting the atmosphere because it is very expensive to clean up.

(B) The Clear Skies project will create a healthier country because people will stop breathing in fine particles and pollutants.

(C) People are dying from the fact that we are allowing them to exist in an unhealthy world.

(D) Both people and the environment will benefit from our efforts to clean up our atmosphere.

5 Which of the following is the best title for this passage?

(A) Clean Skies Saves Lives and Money

(B) Enough of Polluted Skies

(C) Save Our National Parks

(D) Don't Wait Until 2020

6 The word <u>incorrigible</u> most nearly means

(A) substantial.

(B) unmanageable.

(C) wise.

(D) timely.

7 The root word in <u>contrary</u> means

(A) with.

(B) outside.

(C) against.

(D) evidence.

8 The word <u>malleable</u> most nearly means

(A) adaptable.

(B) significant.

(C) horrific.

(D) honorable.

9 The word that means most nearly the opposite of <u>fallacious</u> is

(A) wonderful.

(B) immense.

(C) true.

(D) error.

10 The definition of <u>antithesis</u> is

(A) the exact opposite.

(B) a wonderful thought.

(C) hard to control.

(D) a clown act.

11 The suffix <u>-er</u> in the word *bigger* means

(A) exempt in.

(B) less of.

(C) ending with.

(D) more of.

12 Which word is the correct one to use in this sentence?

The only problem with living in that area was that there were <u>less/fewer</u> days of sunshine.

(A) less

(B) fewer

13 Is the following sentence fact or opinion?

If the writer who ventures to say something more about books and their uses is wise, he will not begin with an apology; for he will know that, despite all that has been said and written on this engrossing theme, the interest of books is inexhaustible.

(A) Fact

(B) Opinion

⑭ Which word is the correct one to use in this sentence?

Mary's prized plant died/dyed because of the unexpected freeze.

Ⓐ died

Ⓑ dyed

Read the following paragraph and answer questions 15 and 16.

In a time when only the moon and the stars lit up the night sky, fear and foreboding rose whenever a blood-red dot looped its way across an otherwise still sky. Mars, the Red Planet, was a familiar and yet suspicious omen, a symbol for war and aggression for thousands of years.

⑮ What mood is the author trying to convey?

Ⓐ Sadness

Ⓑ Menace

Ⓒ Joy

Ⓓ Calm

⑯ Which statement best paraphrases the paragraph?

Ⓐ Ever since man saw the red planet, they ached to visit one day.

Ⓑ For early man, the red planet was a symbol of war and devastation.

Ⓒ Man considered Mars to be an intruder in the night sky and they were suspicious of it.

Ⓓ Mars created a level of unsettling apprehension when the planet appeared in the night sky.

AFQT Posttest

Read the passage and answer questions 17–19.

Allan Pinkerton, founder of Pinkerton's National Detective Agency, was one of the most original and successful detectives in our history. Pinkerton emigrated to the United States and eventually established a barrel-making shop in a small town outside of Chicago. His shop functioned as a "station" for escaped slaves traveling the Underground Railroad to freedom in the North.

Pinkerton's career as a detective began by chance when he discovered a gang of counterfeiters operating in an area where he was gathering wood. His assistance—first in arresting these men and then another counterfeiter—led to his appointment as deputy and, later, as Chicago's first full-time detective.

Pinkerton left his job with the Chicago police force to start his own detective agency. One of the first of its kind, this predecessor to Pinkerton's National Detective Agency provided an array of private detective services, specializing in the capture of train robbers and counterfeiters, and in providing private security services for a variety of industries. By the end of his career, Pinkerton's growing agency had accumulated an extensive collection of criminal dossiers and mug shots that became a model for other police forces.

17 Which of the following statements can be inferred from this passage?

Ⓐ Pinkerton was an excellent business owner in the Chicago area.

Ⓑ Pinkerton posted mug shots of criminals at the local post office so that others could help in their capture.

Ⓒ Pinkerton did not support slavery.

Ⓓ Pinkerton did not believe in carrying guns.

18 In the passage, the following events occurred. Place them in the order in which they happened.

1. Pinkerton emigrates to the United States.
2. Pinkerton starts his own detective agency.
3. Pinkerton becomes a full-time detective.
4. Pinkerton starts a barrel-making business.

Ⓐ 1,2,3,4,

Ⓑ 1,3,2,4

Ⓒ 2,1,4,3

Ⓓ 1,4,3,2

19 Which of the following sentences in the paragraph best represents the main idea?

Ⓐ By the end of his career, Pinkerton's growing agency had accumulated an extensive collection of criminal dossiers and mug shots that became a model for other police forces.

Ⓑ Allan Pinkerton, founder of Pinkerton's National Detective Agency, was one of the most original and successful detectives in our history.

Ⓒ Pinkerton left his job with the Chicago police force to start his own detective agency.

Ⓓ Pinkerton emigrated to the United States and eventually established a barrel-making shop in a small town outside of Chicago.

Read the following passage and answer questions 20–22.

The flu is a contagious respiratory illness caused by influenza viruses. It can cause mild to severe illness, and at times can lead to death. There are two types of flu that are worrying health workers: the seasonal flu and H1N1 or swine flu. Fortunately, vaccinations have been developed for both types of flu.

Some people, such as older people, young children, pregnant women, and people with certain health conditions (such as asthma, diabetes, or heart disease), are at increased risk for serious complications from seasonal flu illness. H1N1 has been more devastating to young people, as they have not built an immunity to this virus. People over 60 do not seem to be as susceptible to the H1N1 virus.

Spread of the 2009 H1N1 virus is thought to have occurred in the same way that seasonal flu spreads. Flu viruses are spread mainly from person to person through coughing or sneezing by people with influenza. Sometimes people may become infected by touching something—such as a surface or object—with flu viruses on it and then touching their mouth or nose.

20 Which of the following can be concluded from the passage?

Ⓐ A good way to stay protected from the flu is to get a vaccination.

Ⓑ Young people do not need to worry about the seasonal flu.

Ⓒ Your chances of getting the flu increase if you have heart or kidney disease.

Ⓓ Don't cough or sneeze near people who have the flu.

21 According to the paragraph which of the following is true?

Ⓐ Young people are more likely to catch the H1N1 flu than the seasonal flu.

Ⓑ Both seasonal flu and H1N1 can be contracted through human contact.

Ⓒ People over 65 are more likely to have serious complications with the H1N1 virus.

Ⓓ Pregnant women and those with chronic illness should not get the flu vaccine.

22 What is the most likely reason the author wrote this passage?

Ⓐ Entertain

Ⓑ Document

Ⓒ Inform

Ⓓ Create fear

AFQT Posttest

The remaining questions are math questions.

23 Find the sum of the following numbers.

    3,357
    4,987
    9,986
      254
  + 12,558

  Ⓐ 29,152
  Ⓑ 29,552
  Ⓒ 30,642
  Ⓓ 31,142

24 Multiply the following numbers.

    785,099 × 5,689 =

  Ⓐ 4,466,428,211
  Ⓑ 4,466,426,211
  Ⓒ 4,476,438,211
  Ⓓ 4,498,428,211

25 Divide the following numbers.

    2,421,243 ÷ 37 =

  Ⓐ 65,439
  Ⓑ 66,439
  Ⓒ 65,739
  Ⓓ 65,449

26 Subtract the following numbers.

    − 998
    − 776

  Ⓐ − 222
  Ⓑ +222
  Ⓒ −1774
  Ⓓ +1774

27 Round this number to the nearest hundredth.

    345,681.0092

  Ⓐ 345681.00
  Ⓑ 345700
  Ⓒ 345681.01
  Ⓓ 345680

28 Solve the following problem.

    $(10)^2 - (9)^2 - 12 + 3^2 =$

  Ⓐ 156
  Ⓑ 16
  Ⓒ −23
  Ⓓ −16

29 Express this fraction in lowest terms.

    $\dfrac{224}{1792} =$

  Ⓐ $\dfrac{2}{4}$

  Ⓑ $\dfrac{3}{5}$

  Ⓒ $\dfrac{9}{12}$

  Ⓓ $\dfrac{1}{8}$

30 Change $\dfrac{87}{5}$ into a mixed number.

  Ⓐ $87\dfrac{1}{5}$

  Ⓑ $85\dfrac{2}{5}$

  Ⓒ $17\dfrac{2}{5}$

  Ⓓ $17\dfrac{3}{5}$

31 Subtract the following.

158.65
−78.97

Ⓐ 81.78
Ⓑ 79.68
Ⓒ 47.98
Ⓓ 45.68

32 What is the solution to the following problem?

$$5\frac{6}{7} \times 4\frac{1}{3} =$$

Ⓐ $20\frac{7}{8}$

Ⓑ $20\frac{4}{21}$

Ⓒ $22\frac{6}{7}$

Ⓓ $25\frac{8}{21}$

33 What is the fraction equivalent of 92%?

Ⓐ $\frac{92}{1,000}$

Ⓑ $\frac{46}{100}$

Ⓒ $\frac{23}{25}$

Ⓓ $\frac{92}{25}$

34 Which of the following is the square root of 529?

Ⓐ 23
Ⓑ 25
Ⓒ 27
Ⓓ 37

35 6.789×10^{-6} is the same as which of the following?

Ⓐ 678,900
Ⓑ 6,789,000
Ⓒ 0.00006789
Ⓓ 0.000006789

36 Sally is training for a marathon. During the first week of training, she runs 10 mi on day 1, 12.5 mi on day 2, 15 mi on day 5, and 17 mi on day 6. Which is closest to the average distance she ran on those days she trained?

Ⓐ 9.08 mi
Ⓑ 12.66 mi
Ⓒ 13.63 mi
Ⓓ 15.54 mi

37 The chart below shows the percent of the population in various regions that regularly use the Internet. In which region do about 50% of the people regularly use the Internet?

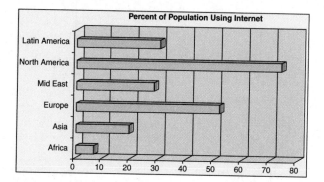

Ⓐ Latin America
Ⓑ Europe
Ⓒ Asia
Ⓓ Mid East

38 Solve the following equation for z.

$z + 4j = 33 + j + k$

Ⓐ $z = 33 - 3j + k$
Ⓑ $z = 30 - j + k$
Ⓒ $z = 33 - 4j + k$
Ⓓ $z = 33 - k + 4j$

39 Jacob has a $5,000 loan that needs to be paid off with 8% interest after a year. How much will he pay in interest in addition to his loan?

Ⓐ $150
Ⓑ $400
Ⓒ $475
Ⓓ $525

40 A bookshelf can hold 18 equal-width books for every 3 linear feet. How many books can it hold in 50 linear feet?

Ⓐ 150
Ⓑ 220
Ⓒ 300
Ⓓ 425

41 Sam has traveled 800 miles in 1.5 days. How long would it take him to make a cross-country trip of 2,500 miles traveling at the same average speed?

Ⓐ 3.45 days
Ⓑ 4.69 days
Ⓒ 4.98 days
Ⓓ 5.12 days

42 Due to recent heavy rains, the Swanee River is now at flood stage. The normal level is 15 feet, but over the last week, the river has risen by 55%. How many feet has the river risen?

Ⓐ 8.25 feet
Ⓑ 9.0 feet
Ⓒ 9.36 feet
Ⓓ 10.0 feet

43 Wade has a bag full of candies. There are 76 red ones, 92 green ones, 110 yellow ones, 79 blue ones, 145 orange ones, and 98 purple ones. If he draws a candy from the bag without looking, what is the probability that he will draw either a green or purple candy?

Ⓐ 12%
Ⓑ 23%
Ⓒ 27%
Ⓓ 32%

AFQT Posttest

44. In the figure below, angle *CBD* measures 43 degrees. What is the measure of angle *ABD*?

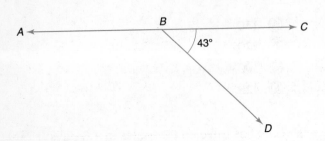

A. 7°
B. 37°
C. 47°
D. 137°

45. The figure below is an isosceles triangle and angle *a* measures 32°. What is the measure of angle *b*?

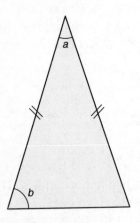

A. 32°
B. 58°
C. 66°
D. 74°

46. In the rectangle below, what is the measure of angle *ABC*?

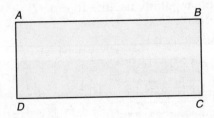

A. 45°
B. 90°
C. 180°
D. 360°

47. Frederico and Darian are creating a garden in their backyard. The garden has the shape of a parallelogram with the short side measuring 1.6 m and the long side measuring 2.7 m. How many meters of fencing do they have to place around the edge of the garden to keep out the local animals?

A. 4.3 m
B. 5.3 m
C. 8.6 m
D. 9.6 m

48. Haden and Maura are carpeting their rectangular living room. If the room measures 12 × 15 ft, how many square yards of carpeting do they need?

A. 20 sq yd
B. 54 sq yd
C. 108 sq yd
D. 180 sq yd

49 A dump truck has a capacity of 2,640 cubic feet. Which of the following could be the measurements of that truck?

Ⓐ 8 ft × 10 ft × 30 ft
Ⓑ 8 ft × 8 ft × 40 ft
Ⓒ 22 ft × 12 ft × 10 ft
Ⓓ 50 ft × 3 ft × 12 ft

50 Jaheem and Jules are planning a circular flower garden for a client. If the diameter is 3 m, what is the area?

Ⓐ 4 m²
Ⓑ 4.7 m²
Ⓒ 5.7 m²
Ⓓ 7.1 m²

STOP. This is the end of the AFQT Posttest. Use the Scoring Sheet on page 160 to check your answers.

Posttest Scoring Sheet

Item	Skill #	Pages in Book	Your Answer	Correct Answer	Correct Y or N
1	13	50–51		C	
2	4	32–33		D	
3	15	54–57		B	
4	2	28–29		D	
5	3	30–31		A	
6	17	62–65		B	
7	14	52–53		C	
8	18	66–69		A	
9	21	78–79		C	
10	19	70–73		A	
11	16	58–61		D	
12	22	80–81		B	
13	20	74–77		A	
14	9	42–43		A	
15	6	36–37		B	
16	10	44–45		D	
17	12	48–49		C	
18	7	38–39		D	
19	1	26–27		B	
20	5	34–35		A	
21	11	46–47		B	
22	8	40–41		C	
23	23	82–83		D	
24	24	84–85		A	
25	25	86–87		A	

Posttest Scoring Sheet

Item	Skill #	Pages in Book	Your Answer	Correct Answer	Correct Y or N
26	26	88–89		C	
27	27	90–91		C	
28	28	92–93		B	
29	29	94–95		D	
30	30	96–97		C	
31	31	98–99		B	
32	32	100–101		D	
33	33	102–103		C	
34	34	104–105		A	
35	35	106–107		D	
36	36	108–109		C	
37	37	110–113		B	
38	38	114–117		A	
39	39	118–119		B	
40	40	120–121		C	
41	41	122–123		B	
42	42	124–125		A	
43	43	126–127		D	
44	44	128–131		D	
45	45	132–135		D	
46	46	136–139		B	
47	47	140–141		C	
48	48	142–145		A	
49	49	146–147		C	
50	50	148–149		D	

Skill Answers and Solutions

Skill 1 (page 27)

Find the Main Idea in a Sentence in the Passage

1. A

2. A or E can be correct answers as they both convey the same general idea.

Skill 2 (page 29)

Choose the Best Summary Statement of the Main Idea

1. C

2. D

3. B

Skill 3 (page 31)

Identify the Best Title

1. Possible Answers: "Winning Hispanic Athletes," "Hispanic Winners," "Hispanics in Sports."

2. Possible Answers: "Patriotic Music," "Military Music," "Patriotism through Music."

Skill 4 (page 33)

Focus on Facts and Details

1. D

2. D

3. A

4. B

Skill 5 (page 35)

Draw Conclusions

1. B

2. A

Skill 6 (page 37)

Identify the Feeling or Mood of the Passage

1. D

2. Here are some words you should have circled: wrong, strange, sinister, dimly subtle aura of brooding evil, amazement, a moon weirdly different, baleful green, glowing with a stark malignant fire like that which lurks in the blazing heart of a giant emerald, glow of the intense green rays, desolate eerie beauty.

3. A

4. Here are some words you should have circled: dimpled face, shines like sweet oil, warm firelight, unbroken smile of fun, good humor, fills one's heart with sunshine,

Skill 7 (page 39)

Focus on the Order of Events

1. A

2. I was worried about scoring well on my history test. I found a comfortable place to study and settled in for a long session. Opening my history book to Chapter 12, I started reading. I underlined the important points. After a few hours, I tested my knowledge of dates and people in the Civil War.

Skill 8 (page 41)

Identify the Author's Purpose

1. B; C is a good answer, but not the best one.

2. D

3. Here are some words you could have circled: nerves were on edge, smell of ammonia, faintest of sounds, motion somewhere behind him, muscles were tensing, flung himself wildly, big and dark, slapped heavily down.

Skill Answers and Solutions

Skill 9 (page 43)

Distinguish between Facts and Opinions

1. 1. opinion 2. fact 3. fact 4. opinion
2. 1. opinion 2. fact 3. fact 4. fact 5. opinion
3. 1. opinion 2. fact 3. fact 4. fact

Skill 10 (page 45)

Paraphrase to Understand What You Are Reading

1. **Possible Paraphrase:** Architects are focusing on the pinecone as an example of a material that responds to heat and cold. When the temperature is cold, the pinecone remains tightly closed. When it is warm, it opens to let go it its seeds. This idea can be used to control temperature in a house.

2. **Possible Paraphrase:** On Suspension Day, October 14, banking was stopped. This was in response to the decreasing public faith in the banking systems and financial institutions. The hardest hit areas were in the East, where many banks closed in larger cities like New York, Baltimore and Philadelphia.

Skill 11 (page 47)

Compare and Contrast

1.

Topics	Labradoodle	Portuguese Water Dog
Hypoallergenic?	Yes	Yes
Good with Families?	Yes	Yes
Needs a Lot of Attention	No	Yes
Needs a Lot of Exercise?	No	Yes
New Breed of Dog	Yes	No

Skill 12 (page 49)

Make Inferences

1. A
2. B

Skill 13 (page 51)

Use Context Clues to Understand Unfamiliar Words

1. B
2. B
3. C
4. D
5. C
6. A

Skill Answers and Solutions

Skill 14 (page 53)

Know Root Words

1. cardiologist (heart doctor); cardiac (relating to the heart) cardiopulmonary (pertaining to the heart and lungs); cardiology (study of the heart)

2. chronological (in order of time); chronic (lasting a long time); synchronize (happening at the same time)

3. incline (a surface that leans or slopes); recline (lean back)

4. incognito (disguised so no one knows you); recognize (to discover that you know someone or something)

5. bicycle (a two-wheeled vehicle); cycle (something that is repeated); cyclone (a storm with circling winds)

6. dental (relating to teeth); dentist (tooth doctor)

7. geography (study of the Earth's surface); geology (study of the structure of the Earth)

8. international (involving two or more countries); intersection (place where roads come together); intermurals (contest between two teams from different organizations)

9. illuminate (fill with light); luminous (radiating or reflecting light)

10. microbe (very small living thing); microchip (a tiny computer wafer); microscope (a device to see very small things)

11. omnipotent (having all the power); omniscient (knowing all things); omnivorous (eating all foods)

12. podiatrist (foot doctor); podium (small platform to stand on); tripod (a stand with three legs)

Skill 15 (page 56)

Recognize Prefixes and Their Meanings

Prefix	Meaning	Words That Include the Prefix (possible answers)
anti-	opposing, against, the opposite	antipathy, antiwar, antisocial
circum-	around	circumvent, circumnavigate
counter-	opposition, opposite direction	counterattack, counterclockwise
dis-	remove, negate	disengage, discord, discomfort
dys-	ill, difficult, bad	dysentery, dyslexia
extra-	outside, beyond	extraordinary, extracurricular
in-/im-	into	influence, influx, imbibe, import
inter-	between	interact, interchange
micro-	small	microelectronics, microscope
macro-	large	macrobiotics, macrocosm
mono-	one, single	monotheism, monarchy, monogamy
over-	excessively, completely	overgrown, overprotective
over-	on top of, above	overshoe, overalls
poly-	many, several	polygamy, polytechnic, polytheism
post-	after	postoperative, posthumous, postpone
pro-	favoring, in support of/ before	promote, project, profess
proto-	first	protozoa, protoplasm
pseudo-	false	pseudonym
re-	again	recede, regress, reproduce
retro-	back	retrograde, retrospective
sub-	under	submarine, subway, subterranean
trans-	across	transpose, transfer
ultra-	beyond, extreme	ultraviolet, ultrasonic

Skill Answers and Solutions

Skill 16 (page 60)

Recognize Suffixes and Their Meanings

Suffix	Meaning	Words That Include the Suffix (possible answers)
-able	able to be	excitable, portable, noticeable
-acity (-ocity)	quality of	perspicacity, sagacity
-age	action or process	passage, pilgrimage, voyage
-ance	state or quality of	defiance, annoyance
-ate	makes it a verb	activate, evaporate, medicate
-crat	person with power	aristocrat, technocrat
-er	more	faster, happier, harder
-escence	condition, state or process	convalescence
-est	most	funniest, silliest, holiest
-ible	able to be	edible, combustible, perceptible
-ish	like something	childish, selfish, bookish
-less	without	fearless, helpless
-like	similar to/ resembling	warlike, ghostlike
-ly	in the manner of	scholarly, wildly, happily
-ology	study of	anthropology, archaeology, technology, physiology
-or	person who	legislator, translator
-phobia	fear of	claustrophobia, xenophobia
-ship	having the skill of	citizenship, friendship
-ular	relating to or resembling	cellular, circular
-ward	in the direction of	forward, eastward, westward, outward

Skill 17 (page 63)

Identify Synonyms—Part 1

1. A
2. A
3. D
4. B
5. D
6. A
7. D
8. A
9. C
10. B
11. A
12. A
13. D
14. C
15. A
16. B
17. D
18. B
19. C
20. A

Skill Answers and Solutions

Skill 18 (page 67)

Identify Synonyms—Part 2

Word	Meaning	Synonym(s)
astonishing	astounding	amazing, remarkable
systematic	orderly	methodical, organized
conscientious	careful	meticulous, painstaking
fundamental	basic	elemental, essential, underlying
observation	inspection	scrutiny, notice, watching, regarding
maneuver	scheme	tactic, ploy, strategy
undoubtedly	certainly	unquestionably, definitely
influential	powerful	important, mighty
corresponding	matching	equivalent, comparable
mischievous	playful	roguish, teasing
interpretation	explanation	translation, clarification
sacrilegious	irreverent	disrespectful, profane
repetition	repeating	recurrence, copying
incredulous	disbelieving	doubtful, questioning
prevalent	common	widespread, abundant
inflammable	able to burn	combustible
synthesis	mixture	combination
privilege	special right	exemption, immunity, prerogative
opposition	resistance	disagreement, antagonism, hostility
conjunction	combination	union, alliance, joining
treacherous	disloyal	underhanded, untrustworthy
recognition	identification	acknowledgment, appreciation
preference	penchant	inclination, choice, selection
strenuous	laborious	arduous, difficult, wearying
annoyance	irritation	bother, disturbance, aggravation
tendency	inclination	trend, propensity, bent
accumulate	gather	amass, collect, assemble
courteous	polite	considerate, respectful, mannerly
analogous	corresponding	similar, alike, proportionate
temperament	personality	disposition, behavior, character
tranquility	serenity	peacefulness, calmness
perseverance	persistence	resolve, tenacity
obstacle	impediment	hindrance, obstruction, blockage
permissible	allowed	tolerated, legitimate, permitted
accessible	available	obtainable, understandable
haphazard	random	chaotic, disorganized, irregular
feasible	possible	viable, practical, workable
intervene	come between	intercede, mediate
cynical	skeptical	doubting, distrusting
discriminate	distinguish	classify, divide, differentiate
melancholy	sad	downhearted, mournful, distressed
illogical	irrational	unsound, unreasonable
sufficient	enough	full, adequate, passable, satisfactory
symmetrical	balanced	even, proportional, harmonious
tyranny	oppression	domination, repression, despotism

Skill Answers and Solutions

Skill 19 (page 71)

Build Your Vocabulary

Word	Definition
abominable	extremely repugnant or offensive
abrasion	the process of wearing away by friction
acrimonious	full of or displaying anger and resentment; bitter
adjudicate	to make an official decision about a problem or dispute
affiliate	to join a group or idea; associate; partner
allegiance	loyalty to or support for a person, cause, or group
altruism	acting with unselfish concern for others
ambivalent	having mixed feelings; uncertain or unsure
belligerent	hostile, ready to start a fight, or ready to go to war
blatant	obtrusive and conspicuous in an offensive way; obvious
boisterous	full of noisy enthusiasm and energy; lively; energetic
cadence	the beat or measure of something such as a dance or a march that follows a set rhythm
cessation	a stop, pause, or interruption; termination; end
circuitous	roundabout; indirect; meandering
coalition	union between two or more groups; alliance; merger
compatible	able to exist, live, or work together without conflict
concentric	describing circles and spheres of different sizes with the same middle point
confiscate	to take somebody's property with authority
consensus	general or widespread agreement among all the members of a group; accord; harmony
courteous	polite in a way that shows consideration of others; considerate
culpable	deserving blame or punishment for a wrong; guilty
deteriorate	to become or make something worse in quality, value, or strength
disseminate	to distribute or spread something, especially information
eccentric	unconventional, especially in a whimsical way
emancipate	to free somebody from slavery, serfdom, or other forms of bondage
enumerate	to name a number of things on a list one by one; itemize
eradicate	to destroy or get rid of something completely, so that it can never recur or return
exacerbate	to make an already bad or problematic situation worse
facsimile	an exact copy or reproduction of something
forfeit	to give something up
formidable	inspiring respect or wonder because of size, strength, or ability; difficult to overcome
germane	properly related to something, especially something being discussed; relevant; pertinent
gullible	tending to trust and believe people, and therefore easily tricked or deceived

Skill Answers and Solutions

Word	Definition
hesitant	slow to do or say something because of indecision or lack of confidence
impetus	the energy or motivation to accomplish or undertake something; thrust; force
incentive	something that encourages or motivates somebody to do something
incinerate	to burn to ashes, or cause something to burn to ashes; destroy; cremate
incongruous	unsuitable or out of place in a specific setting or context; incompatible
insinuate	hint at something unpleasant or suggest it indirectly and gradually; imply; hint
jeopardize	to put somebody or something at risk of being lost, harmed, killed, or destroyed; endanger
latent	present or existing, but in an underdeveloped form; in the background; hidden; underlying
legacy	something that is handed down or remains from a previous generation or time; heritage
legitimate	complying with recognized rules, standards, or traditions; lawful; valid; justifiable
magnanimous	very generous, kind, or forgiving; fair; noble
mediate	to work with both sides in a dispute in an attempt to help them to reach an agreement; referee; intercede
menace	a possible source of danger or harm; threat; hazard
morbid	showing a strong interest in unpleasant or gloomy subjects such as death, murder, or accidents; gloomy; dark
nebulous	not clear, distinct, or definite; hazy; vague
negligent	habitually careless or irresponsible; remiss; slipshod; lax
obtrusive	highly noticeable, often with a bad or unwelcome effect; conspicuous
oscillate	to swing between two points with a rhythmic motion; unable to decide between two things; vacillate; wavering
ostracize	to banish or exclude somebody from a particular group, either formally or informally; shun; snub
panacea	a supposed cure for all diseases or problems; universal remedy
perennial	constantly recurring, or lasting for an indefinite time; recurrent; returning; perpetual
perilous	involving exposure to very great danger; dangerous; hazardous
perishable	liable to decay, rot, or spoil; consumable; fragile
pertinent	relevant to the matter being considered
pinnacle	the highest or topmost point or level of something; summit; top; apex
precedent	an established custom or practice; example; model
predominant	most common or greatest in number or amount; most important, powerful, or influential
premonition	a strong feeling, without a rational basis, that something is going to happen
prominent	distinguished, eminent, or well-known; famous
propensity	a tendency to demonstrate particular behavior; tendency; inclination
proximity	closeness in space or time; nearness
ratify	to give formal approval to something; approve; endorse
recalcitrant	stubbornly resisting the authority of another person or group; difficult to deal with; stubborn
reconcile	to solve a dispute or end a quarrel; settle; bring together; patch up
refurbish	to bring something back to a cleaner, brighter, or more functional state; restore; renovate

Skill Answers and Solutions

Word	Definition
reminisce	to talk or write about events remembered from the past; recall; recollect
rescind	to declare a decision or enactment null and void; withdraw; repeal; cancel
resilient	able to recover quickly from setbacks; flexible; elastic
retaliate	to deliberately harm somebody in response or revenge for a harm to you; get revenge
sanguine	cheerfully optimistic; positive; upbeat
sedentary	involving a lot of sitting and correspondingly little exercise; inactive
simultaneous	done, happening, or existing at the same time; concurrent; real-time
sleuth	a person who makes investigations; detective
spontaneous	arising from natural impulse or inclination, rather than from planning or in response to suggestions from others; impulsive
sporadic	occurring at intervals that have no apparent pattern; irregular; intermittent; periodic
squalid	neglected, unsanitary and unpleasant; filthy; nasty
stringent	strictly controlled or enforced; strict; rigorous; harsh
superfluous	not essential; extra; surplus; unnecessary; unneeded
susceptible	easily influenced or affected by something; vulnerable; at risk; predisposed
taut	pulled or stretched tightly; tense; rigid; firm
tenacious	tending to stick firmly to any decision, plan, or opinion without changing or doubting it; strong; stubborn; obstinate
tenuous	not based on anything significant or substantial, and therefore unlikely to stand up to rigorous examination; fragile; easily broken
testimonial	a favorable report on the qualities and virtues of somebody or something; tribute
trajectory	the path that a projectile makes through space under the action of given forces such as thrust, wind, and gravity; path route; course
translucent	allowing light to pass through, but only diffusely, so that objects on the other side cannot be clearly distinguished
trepidation	fear or uneasiness about the future or a future event; anxiety; unease; apprehension
truncate	to shorten something by cutting off or removing a part; abbreviate; cut
tumultuous	noisy and unrestrained in a way that shows excitement or great happiness; turbulent; riotous
ubiquitous	present everywhere at once, or seeming to be; everywhere; omnipresent
vicarious	experienced through somebody else rather than at first hand
voracious	desiring or consuming something in great quantities; avid; insatiable
whimsical	imaginative and impulsive; fanciful; amusing

Skill Answers and Solutions

Skill 20 (page 75)

Know (No) Homonyms

1. A
2. B
3. B
4. A
5. B
6. A
7. B
8. A
9. B
10. B
11. B
12. B
13. A
14. B
15. B
16. A
17. A
18. B
19. A
20. B
21. A
22. B
23. A
24. A
25. A

Skill 21 (page 79)

Know Antonyms

Word	Antonym
entrance	exit
excited	calm
export	import
feeble	strong
freedom	captivity
frank	secretive
generous	selfish
gloomy	cheerful
harmless	dangerous
hasten	dawdle
horizontal	vertical
inferior	superior
intentional	accidental
loyal	disloyal
maximize	minimize
minority	majority
optimist	pessimist
permanent	temporary
sorrow	joy
success	failure
transparent	opaque
vacant	occupied
voluntary	compulsory

Skill Answers and Solutions

Skill 22 (page 80)

Watch for Words That Are Often Confused

1. B
2. A
3. B
4. A
5. A
6. B
7. B
8. B
9. A
10. B
11. A
12. A
13. B
14. A
15. C

Skill 23 (page 82)

Add and Subtract Accurately

1. 12
2. 15
3. 12
4. 17
5. 29
6. 31
7. 95
8. 106
9. 613
10. 1,887

11. 1,459
12. 2,241
13. 16
14. 129
15. 1,548
16. 25
17. 32
18. 1,354
19. 178
20. 1,112
21. 1,127
22. 1,151
23. 1,478
24. 2,809
25. 16,606
26. 12,305
27. 20,394
28. 6,695
29. 5
30. 6
31. 72
32. 200
33. 404
34. 700
35. 309
36. 11
37. 1,819
38. 611
39. 1,790
40. 8,775

Skill Answers and Solutions

Skill 24 (page 84)
Multiply Whole Numbers

1. 36
2. 56
3. 64
4. 72
5. 69
6. 264
7. 615
8. 1,476
9. 4,606
10. 144,243
11. 132
12. 7,722
13. 204,761
14. 247,604
15. 12,799,807

Skill 25 (page 86)
Divide Whole Numbers

1. 56
2. 25
3. 45
4. 5
5. 46
6. 222
7. 37
8. 897
9. 22
10. 468
11. 456
12. 13.6

13. 33.33
14. 40.75
15. 27
16. 111.75
17. 204
18. 116.17
19. 185.33
20. 2,739
21. 689
22. 914
23. 49
24. 24
25. 31
26. 247
27. 16
28. 19
29. 17
30. 941

Skill 26 (page 89)
Work with Positive and Negative Numbers

1. −15
2. −87
3. −9,998
4. 297
5. −24
6. −348
7. 18
8. 1,455
9. −27
10. −148
11. −22

Skill Answers and Solutions

12. 22

13. −25

14. −500

15. −500

Skill 27 (page 91)
Know Place Values and How to Round

1. 356,890
2. 100,000.5
3. 845,000
4. 234,592,000
5. 234,590,000
6. 235,000,000
7. 557,456.1
8. 557,500
9. 455.9
10. 455.88

Skill 28 (page 93)
Order Your Operations

1. 100
2. 19.75
3. 12
4. 30
5. 2
6. $144 + 18 = 162$
7. $196 + 9 = 205$
8. $8 + 3 − 10 = 1$
9. $16 − 9 + 3 = 10$
10. $4 + 4 − 13 = −5$
11. $125 − 4 − 15 + 14 = 120$
12. $(4 + 16 − 10)^2 = 10^2 = 100$

Skill 29 (page 95)
Use Fractions and Decimals

1. $\frac{1}{4}$
2. $\frac{1}{3}$
3. $\frac{1}{16}$
4. $\frac{1}{20}$
5. 0.25
6. 0.33
7. 0.0625
8. 0.05
9. $\frac{3}{4}$
10. $\frac{9}{40}$

Skill 30 (page 97)
Understand Mixed Numbers

1. $\frac{41}{8}$
2. $\frac{21}{2}$
3. $\frac{50}{3}$
4. $\frac{79}{8}$
5. $5\frac{1}{8}$
6. $10\frac{1}{2}$
7. $16\frac{2}{3}$
8. $9\frac{7}{8}$
9. $\frac{87}{4} = 21.75$
10. $\frac{545}{6} = 90.83$

Skill Answers and Solutions

Skill 31 (page 99)

Add and Subtract Fractions, Mixed Numbers, and Decimals

1. $\frac{9}{6} = 1\frac{3}{6} = 1\frac{1}{2}$

2. $\frac{8}{12} + \frac{9}{12} = \frac{17}{12} = 1\frac{5}{12}$

3. $\frac{14}{18} - \frac{9}{18} = \frac{5}{18}$

4. $27\frac{4}{6} + 5\frac{5}{6} = 33 + \frac{3}{6} = 33\frac{1}{2}$

5. $27\frac{4}{6} - 5\frac{5}{6} = \frac{166}{6} - \frac{35}{6} = \frac{131}{6} = 21\frac{5}{6}$

6. 99.86

7. 33.46

8. $4\frac{5}{8}$

9. $-2\frac{1}{8}$

10. 958.47

11. 4,484.32711

12. 38.287423

13. 0.06032

14. 0.065

Skill 32 (page 101)

Multiply and Divide Fractions, Mixed Numbers, and Decimals

1. $\frac{14}{24} = \frac{7}{12}$

2. $\frac{9}{5} \times \frac{20}{7} = \frac{180}{35} = \frac{36}{7} = 5\frac{1}{7}$

3. 35.19

4. $\frac{16}{21}$

5. $\frac{47}{8} \div \frac{9}{4} = \frac{47}{8} \times \frac{4}{9} = \frac{188}{72} = 2\frac{44}{72} = 2\frac{11}{18}$

6. 1.38

7. $1\frac{7}{8}$

8. 16.56

9. $2\frac{8}{15}$

10. 102.87

11. 1.57

12. 3627.164

Skill 33 (page 103)

Convert between Percents, Fractions, and Decimals

1. 0.33

2. 0.625

3. $\frac{33}{100}$

4. $\frac{5}{8}$

5. $\frac{17}{20}$

6. 80%

7. 87.5%

8. 120%

Skill 34 (page 105)

Use Exponents and Roots

1. 16

2. 256

Skill Answers and Solutions

3. 12 or –12

4. 12 or –12

5. 7

6. 36

7. 27

8. 9

9. 9

10. 24 or –24

11. $\dfrac{1}{16}$

12. $\dfrac{1}{8}$

Skill 35 (page 107)

Use Scientific Notation

1. 6,770,000

2. 0.00000677

3. 8.77×10^{-6}

4. 8.77×10^{-12}

5. 1.233344×10^{21}

6. 6.6×10^{15}

7. 2.0×10^{2}

Skill 36 (page 109)

Identify and Understand the Mean, Median, and Mode

1. $500 \div 10 = 50$

2. $967 \div 11 = 87.9$

3. 82

4. $(82 + 76) \div 2 = 79$

5. 50

6. 50 and 76

Skill 37 (page 112)

Interpret Charts and Graphs

1. 74

2. Sal

3. 300

4. About 29%

5. 91

6. Weeks 5 and 10

7. 50

8. B

9. D

Skill 38 (page 117)

Understand and Solve Equations

1. $5x = 25$; $x = 5$

2. $7x = 49$; $x = 7$

3. $40x = 1200$; $x = 30$

4. $3y = 4x$; $y = \dfrac{(4x)}{3}$

5. $9y - 3y = 24$; $6y = 24$; $y = 4$

6. $kl = jm$; $k = \dfrac{(jm)}{1}$

7. $x^2 + 10x + 21$

8. $j^2 + 4j - 12$

9. $(c + 10)(c - 2)$

10. $(g - 8)(g + 2)$

Skill 39 (page 119)

Calculate Simple and Compound Interest

1. $\$1500 \times 0.025 = \$37.50$; balance will be $\$1,537.50$.

2. Year 1: $\$2,200 \times 0.03 = \$66$

   Year 2: $\$2,266 \times 0.03 = \$67.98$

   Year 3: $\$2,333.98 \times 0.03 = \$70.02$

   Year 4: $\$2,404 \times 0.03 = \$72.12 = \$2,476.12$

3. Year 5

Skill Answers and Solutions

Skill 40 (page 121)

Use Ratio and Proportion to Solve Problems

1. $\dfrac{850}{x} = \dfrac{3500}{1} = 0.24$ lb

2. $\dfrac{350}{1} = \dfrac{x}{4.2} =$

   $x = 1,470 \times 2$ weeks $= 2,940$ calories

3. Change hours into minutes; 2 hours = 120 minutes and then set up the proportion.

   $\dfrac{34}{3} = \dfrac{x}{120}$

   $3x = 4,080$

   $x = 1,360$ boxes

4. $\dfrac{105}{1} = \dfrac{1190}{x} =$

   $105x = 1,190$

   $x = 11.33$

5. 6.5 hours $\times$ 14 = 91 crates

6. $\dfrac{250}{1.5} = \dfrac{x}{6} =$

   $1.5x = 1500$

   $x = 1000$ square feet

Skill 41 (page 123)

Calculate Distance, Rate, and Time

1. 125 miles/hour $\times$ 8.75 hours = 1,093.75 miles

2. 68 ÷ 45 = 1.51 hours

3. 384,403 km ÷ 5 days = 76,880.6 km/day ÷ 24 = 3,203.36 km/hr

4. 14 $\times$ 45 = 630 miles

5. 2790 miles ÷ 55 = 50.73 miles/day

Skill 42 (page 125)

Determine Change and Percent Change

1. $\dfrac{14 \text{ inches}}{55 \text{ inches}} = 0.2545$ or 25%

2. $25\% = \dfrac{x}{54} = 0.25 \times 54° = 13.5°$. Subtract from 54 to get 40.5°.

3. $55\% = \dfrac{x}{\$35} = 0.55 \times \$35 = \$19.25$ increase in price, bringing the total cost to $35 + $19.25 = $54.25

4. 2,500,000 ÷ 500,000 = 0.2 = 20%

5. $1700 $\times$ 0.30 = $510; $1700 − $510 = $1190

6. 25 ft $\times$ 0.40 = 10 ft; 25 ft + 10 ft = 35 ft.

Skill 43 (page 127)

Calculate the Probability of an Event

1. There are 1,000 possible outcomes. Rock + Country = 590 positive outcomes, so
   Probability $= \dfrac{590}{1000} = \dfrac{59}{100} = 0.59$ or 59%

2. Probability $= \dfrac{890}{1,000} = \dfrac{89}{100} = 0.89$ or 89%

3. Probability $= \dfrac{2}{8} = \dfrac{1}{4} = 0.25$ or 25%

Skill 44 (page 130)

Analyze Lines and Angles

1. 68°

2. 128°

3. $\angle ABE = 73°$ $\angle ABC = 107°$

4. $\angle LMY = 50°$ so $\angle JMG = 50°$

5. 140°

6. 140°

7. 40°

8. 40°

Skill Answers and Solutions

Skill 45 (page 135)

Understand the Characteristics of Triangles

1. $\angle x$ is 105°, so side c is the longest.

2. 75°

3. c^2 = 130 or c is about 11.4 cm

Skill 46 (page 138)

Know the Characteristics of Quadrilaterals

1. All the angles measure 90°.

2. 34 + 34 = 68; 360 − 68 = 292; $\frac{1}{2}$ of 292 = 146, so angle b measures 146°.

3. C

4. 55°

5. 90°

Skill 47 (page 141)

Calculate the Perimeter of Polygons

1. 4.3 + 4.3 + 1.7 + 1.7 = 12 m at $10 = $120

2. 2 sides of 10 ft = 10 × 12 in = 120 in × 2 sides = 240 in

   2 sides of 13 ft 6 in = 13 × 12 in = 156 in + 6 in = 162 in × 2 = 324 in

   Total Amount = 240 in + 324 in = 564 in of molding.

Skill 48 (page 144)

Calculate the Area of Polygons

1. 12 × 20 = 240 ft². 240 ÷ 200 = 1.2 gallons of paint

2. $\frac{1}{2}b \times h = \frac{1}{2}18 \times 12 = \frac{1}{2}(216)$ or 108 m².

   108 ÷ 10 = 10.8 lb; 11 packages.

3. 150 ft²

4. 56 × 16 = 896 m²

5. 896 ÷ 4 = 224 m²/hr

6. 14 × 28 = 392 ft²

7. 392 ÷ 4 = 98 ft²/hr

8. 32 m²

9. 6 × 32 = 192 plants

10. 5 ft × 6 ft = 30 ft²

11. 7 ft × 8 ft = 56 ft²

Skill 49 (page 147)

Calculate the Volume and Surface Area of Solids

1. 6 × 18 × 9 = 972 in³; 972 in³ ÷ 512 = 1.898 or about 1.9 gallons of water.

2. 36 in × 18 in × 24 in = 15,552 in³. If you got this wrong, did you change 1 yd to 36 in?

3. 9 in × 11 in × 24 in = 2,376 in³.

4. This is a question on surface area using Surface Area = 2(lh) + 2(lw) + 2(wh). So 2(6 × 8) + 2(6 × 12) + 2(8 × 12) = 2(48) + 2(72) + 2(96) = 96 + 144 + 192 = 432 cm².

5. 960 cubic feet

Skill 50 (page 149)

Calculate the Measures of a Circle, a Sphere, or a Cylinder

1. If the radius is 0.25 miles, the diameter is 0.5 miles. The circumference is 3.14 × 0.5 = 1.57 miles. Four times around is 6.28 miles.

2. The diameter is 14, so the radius is 7. Using the formula for area, 3.14 × (7)² = 3.14 (49) = 153.86 sq ft or 153.86 ft².

3. The diameter is 8 in, so the radius is 4. The formula is $\frac{4}{3}$ × 3.14 × (4)³ = $\frac{4}{3}$ × 3.14 × 64 = $\frac{4}{3}$ × 200.96 = 267.95 in³ for a single balloon. Multiply by 10 = 2,679.5 in³ for all 10 balloons.

4. V = 3.14 (2)² × 16 = 3.14 × 4 × 16 = 201 in³.

Appendix

AFQT Resources

- Common Word Roots
- Common Prefixes
- Common Suffixes
- Units of Measure
- Fraction, Decimal, and Percent Equivalents
- Geometric Shapes and Formulas
- Key Words in Word Problems

Common Word Roots

Root	Meaning	Examples
act	do	transact, activate
aero	air	aerobics, aerospace
ambu	walk	ambulate, ambulatory
anthrop	human	anthropology, philanthropy
annu, anni	year	annual, anniversary
aster, astr	star	astronomy, asterisk
audi	hear	audible, auditory
biblio	book	bibliography, bibliographic
bio	life	biosphere, biography
brev	short	brevity, abbreviate
capit	head	decapitate, capital
card, cord, cour	heart	cardiology, discord
carn	flesh	carnivorous, carnage
cede	go	recede, precede
chron	time	chronology, synchronize
cide	killing	suicide, homicide
cis	cut	precise, scissors
claim	shout, cry out	exclaim, proclaim
cogn	know	cognition, recognize
crat	rule	autocratic, democrat
culp	blame	culpable, exculpate
dem	people	democracy, demographics
dic, dict	speak	dictation, predict
dorm	sleep	dormant, dormitory
fer	carry	transfer, refer
fuge	flee	refuge, centrifugal
geo	earth	geography, geologic
gram	something written or recorded	telegram, cardiogram
graph	to write	graphic, calligraphy
jac, ject	throw	eject, trajectory
jur	law	jury, jurisprudence
labor	work	laboratory, collaborate
loc	place	location, collocate
luc	light	translucent, illuminate
manu	hand	manuscript, manufacture

Common Word Roots

Root	Meaning	Examples
meter, metr	measure	barometer, metric
morph	form	morphology, amorphous
mort	die	mortuary, mortal
omni	all	omnipresent, omnipotent
op, oper	work	cooperate, operator
path	feeling, suffering	empathy, pathetic
ped, pod	foot	pedal, podiatry
philo, phil	like, love	philanthropy, philosophy
phobe	fear	phobic, claustrophobia
phon	sound	phonograph, stereophonic
photo	light	photographic, telephoto
phys	nature, body	physique, physical
scrib	write	scribble, scribe
stro, stru	build	destroy, construction
ter	earth	extraterrestrial, territory
vac	empty	vacuous, evacuate
verb	word	verbose, proverb
vid, vis	see	video, television
vol, volv	turn, roll	revolve, evolution

Common Prefixes

Prefix	Meaning	Examples
a-, an-	without	amoral, anaerobic
ante-	before	antedate, antechamber
anti-	against, opposing	antipollution, antipathy
auto-	self	autobiography, autopilot
bene-	good or well	beneficial, benediction
bi-	two	bicycle, bipolar
cen-	hundred, hundredth	century, centimeter
circum-	around	circumnavigate, circumvent
co-	together, with	coauthor, copilot
com-	bring together	complete, compile
contra-	against	contradict, contraband
counter-	opposite, against	counterclockwise, counterterrorism
de-	away from, down, undoing	deactivate, detract
dis-	the opposite, undoing	disagree, disarm
ex-	out of, away from	exhale, expropriate
hetero-	different	heterogeneous, heterodox
homo-	same	homogenized, homonym
hyper-	above, excessive	hyperactive, hypertension
il-/in-/ir-	not	illiquid, inaudible, irregular
inter-	between	intercontinental, interject
intra-	within	intramural, intranet
mal-	bad or ill	maladjusted, malevolent
micro-	small	microbiology, microscope
milli-	thousand, thousandth	millennium, millisecond
mis-	bad, wrong	misbehave, misunderstand
mono-	one	monosyllable, monorail
neo-	new	neoclassical, neophyte
non-	not	nonessential, nonconformist
paleo-	old, ancient	paleontology, paleobiology
pan-	all, all over	pandemic, panorama
poly-	many	polygon, polynomial
post-	after, behind	postpone, postnasal
pre-	before	preview, premeditate
pro-	forward, before, in favor of	promote, projection
re-	back, again	rewrite, retract
retro-	backward	retrofit, retroactive
semi-	half	semiannual, semifinal
sub-	under, below	submarine, subway
super-	above, over	supersede, supervise
sym-/syn-	together, at the same time	symbiosis, synchronize
tele-	from a distance	telecommute, telemetry
therm-	heat	thermal, thermometer
tor	twist	torsion, contort
trans-	across	transcontinental, transatlantic
un-	not	unannounced, unnoticed
uni-	one	unicycle, unify
vert, verse	change	revert, reverse

Common Suffixes

Suffix	Meaning	Examples
-able, -ible	capable or worthy of	likable, possible
-ful	full of	healthful, joyful
-fy, -ify	to make or cause	purify, glorify
-ish	like, inclined to, somewhat	impish, devilish
-ism	act of, state of	capitalism, socialism
-ist	one who does	conformist, cyclist
-ize	make into	formalize, legalize
-logue, -log	discourse	dialogue, travelogue
-logy	study of	paleontology, dermatology
-ment	state of being	entertainment, amazement
-oid	like, resembling	humanoid, trapezoid
-ty, -ity	state of being	purity, acidity

Units of Measure

Customary System

Length

12 inches (in) = 1 foot (ft)

3 feet = 1 yard (yd)

36 inches = 1 yard

5,280 feet = 1 mile (mi)

Area

1 square foot (ft^2) = 144 square inches (in^2)

9 square feet = 1 square yard (yd^2)

Weight

16 ounces (oz) = 1 pound (lb)

2,000 pounds = 1 ton

Liquid Volume

2 cups (c) = 1 pint (pt)

2 pints = 1 quart (qt)

4 quarts = 1 gallon (gal)

Time

7 days = 1 week

4 weeks = 1 month

12 months = 1 year

52 weeks = 1 year

10 years = 1 decade

Metric System

Length

100 centimeters (cm) = 1 meter (m)

1,000 meters = 1 kilometer (km)

Volume

1,000 milliliters (mL) = 1 liter (L)

Mass

1,000 grams (g) = 1 kilogram (kg)

1,000 kilograms = 1 metric ton (t)

Converting between Systems

1 meter ≈ 39.37 inches

1 kilometer ≈ 0.62 mile

1 centimeter ≈ 0.39 inch

1 kilogram ≈ 2.2 pounds

1 liter ≈ 1.057 quarts

1 gram ≈ 0.035 ounce

Fraction, Decimal, and Percent Equivalents

Fraction(s)	= Decimal	= Percent (%)
$\frac{1}{100}$	0.01	1%
$\frac{1}{10}$	0.1	10%
$\frac{1}{5} = \frac{2}{10}$	0.2	20%
$\frac{3}{10}$	0.3	30%
$\frac{2}{5} = \frac{4}{10}$	0.4	40%
$\frac{1}{2} = \frac{5}{10}$	0.5	50%
$\frac{3}{5} = \frac{6}{10}$	0.6	60%
$\frac{4}{5} = \frac{8}{10}$	0.8	80%
$\frac{1}{4} = \frac{2}{8} = \frac{25}{100}$	0.25	25%
$\frac{3}{4} = \frac{75}{100}$	0.75	75%
$\frac{1}{3} = \frac{2}{6} = \frac{3}{9}$	0.33	$33\frac{1}{3}\%$
$\frac{2}{3}$	0.66	$66\frac{2}{3}\%$
$\frac{1}{8}$	0.125	12.5%
$\frac{3}{8}$	0.375	37.5%
$\frac{5}{8}$	0.625	62.5%
$\frac{1}{6}$	$0.16\frac{2}{3}$	$16\frac{2}{3}\%$
1	1.00	100%
1.5	1.50	150%

Geometric Shapes and Formulas: Summary

Shapes	Formulas
	Triangle
	Area = $\frac{1}{2}$ of the base × the height
	$A = \frac{1}{2}bh$
	Perimeter = $a + b + c$
	Square
	Area = length × width
	$A = lw$
	Perimeter = side + side + side + side
	$P = 4s$
	Rectangle
	Area = length × width
	$A = lw$
	Perimeter = 2 × length + 2 × width
	$P = 2l + 2w$
	Parallelogram and Rhombus
	Area = base × height
	$A = bh$
	Perimeter = 2 × length + 2 × width
	$P = 2l + 2w$
	Trapezoid
	Area = the sum of the two bases divided by 2 × height
	$A = \left(\dfrac{b_1 + b_2}{2}\right)h$
	$P = a + b_1 + b_2 + c$
	Circle
	The distance around the circle is its circumference (C). The length of a line segment passing through the center with endpoints on the circle is the diameter (d). The length of a line segment connecting the center to a point on the circle is the radius (r). The diameter is twice the length of the radius ($d = 2r$).
	$C = \pi d = 2\pi r$
	$A = \pi r^2$
	$\pi = 3.14$ or $\dfrac{22}{7}$

Geometric Shapes and Formulas: Summary

Shapes	Formulas

Cube

Volume = side × side × side

$V = s^3$

Rectangular Solid

Volume = length × width × height

$V = lwh$

Cylinder

Volume = πr^2 × height

$V = \pi r^2 h$

Sphere

Volume = $\frac{4}{3}\pi r^3$

$V = \frac{4}{3}\pi r^3$

Key Words in Word Problems

Many word problems contain key words that tell you what mathematical operation you need to use to solve the problem. It pays to know these key words, so be sure you study the following list.

Key Words	Example Phrases
	These key words tell you to add.
Increased by	If the temperature is increased by
More than	If the bicycle costs $75 more than
Sum	If the sum of the paychecks is
Total	The total number of payments equals
Added	If *a* is added to *b*
Plus	If the interest plus the principal is
Combined	If the volume of the cube is combined with
In all	How many pounds in all
Successive	The cost of eight successive phone bills
	These key words tell you to subtract.
Less than	The interest payment was less than
Difference	The difference between the time it takes to
Are left	How many pieces of pie are left if
Fewer than	If there are 15 fewer scholarships this year than
Minus	Some number minus 36
Reduced by	If the federal budget is reduced by
	These key words tell you to multiply.
Times	There are three times as many red tiles as blue tiles
Product	The product of a and b is
Increased by a factor of	If the speed is increased by a factor of
Decreased by a factor of	If the temperature is decreased by a factor of
At	If you buy 12 cameras at $249 each
Per	If a ferry can carry 20 cars per trip, how many cars can it carry in 6 trips?
Total	If you spend $10 a week on movies for a total of 5 weeks
Twice	The house covers twice as many square feet as
	These key words tell you to divide.
Quotient	What is the quotient if the numerator is 500?
Divided equally among	If 115 tickets are divided equally among five groups
Divided into equal groups	If the students were divided into six equal groups
Ratio of	If the ratio of oxygen to hydrogen is
Per	If a ferry can carry 24 cars per trip, how many trips will it take to carry 144 cars?
Percent	What percent of 100 is 30?
Half	If half the profits go to charity, then how much
	These key words tell you to use an equal sign.
Is	If the total bill is $19.35
Sells for	If the car sells for $26,000
Gives	If multiplying a^2 and b^2 gives c^2